LANCE ARMSTRONG

HISTORIC SIX-TIME TOUR DE FRANCE CHAMPION

Austin American-Statesman
statesman.com

Sports Publishing L.L.C

www.sportspublishingllc.com

PUBLISHER
Peter L. Bannon

SENIOR MANAGING EDITORS
Joseph J. Bannon and Susan M. Moyer

BOOK DESIGN, BOOK LAYOUT
InnerWorkings, LLC

COORDINATING EDITOR
Noah A. Amstadter

COVER DESIGN
Joseph Brumleve

PHOTO EDITOR
Erin Linden-Levy

Austin American-Statesman
statesman.com

PUBLISHER
Michael Laosa

EDITOR
Richard A. Oppel

EXECUTIVE VICE PRESIDENT AND GENERAL MANAGER
Belinda Gaudet

MANAGING EDITOR
Fred Zipp

VICE PRESIDENT AND CHIEF FINANCIAL OFFICER
Edward Burns

SPORTS EDITOR
John Bridges

DIRECTOR OF PHOTOGRAPHY
Zach Ryall

DESIGN DIRECTOR FOR NEWS
G.W. Babb

"Move over Shaq. There is a new MOST DOMINANT EVER. Shaq's got nothing on Lance. He is the most dominant human being on the face of this earth."

FAN QUOTE

LANCE ARMSTRONG'S TOUR VICTORIES

AMERICAN-STATESMAN STAFF

July 2, 2004

1999
The setup: Armstrong had not competed in the Tour since 1996, when he quit halfway through and was later diagnosed with testicular cancer. Defending champ Marco Pantani was not in the field after getting kicked off the Tour of Italy because of suspected drug use.

Key stage: Armstrong surprised the field by winning the largely ceremonial prologue. More important, he regained the yellow jersey for good in the eighth stage.

Stages won: 4

Biggest deficit: 54 seconds, fifth place, after the seventh stage

Margin of victory: 7 minutes, 37 seconds

Runners-up: Alex Zuelle, Fernando Escartin and Laurent Dufaux.

2000
The setup: Armstrong was one of three past champions in a field that was considerably stronger than 1999. Jan Ullrich, the 1997 winner, was expected to be Armstrong's most formidable challenger.

Key stage: It was a cold, wet day up the Hautacam in the Pyrenees when Armstrong cemented his reputation as a climber. He came in second on the ninth stage but surged into first place in the overall standings.

Stages won: 1

Biggest deficit: 5 minutes, 54 seconds, 16th place, after the eighth stage

**LANCE ARMSTRONG FINISHES THE 17TH STAGE
IN THE 2001 TOUR DE FRANCE, EN ROUTE TO
HIS THIRD STRAIGHT TOUR WIN.**

*"Great jock. Intense.
Dedicated and
disciplined. Competitive
and ambitious."*

FAN QUOTE

Margin of victory: 6 minutes, 2 seconds.

Runners-up: Jan Ullrich, Joseba Beloki, Christophe Moreau.

2001

The setup: If Armstrong was to become the second American to win three Tours, he would have to overcome a huge deficit that continued to grow through the first nine stages. After Stage 8, a victory by Erik Dekker, Armstrong and Jan Ullrich trailed by more than 35 minutes.

Key stage: Armstrong jumped from 23rd to fourth place, making up 15 minutes, with a victory up L'Alpe d'Huez in the 10th stage. The next day, he won a mountain time trial and then took the overall lead in the 13th stage.

Stages won: 4

Biggest deficit: 35 minutes, 19 seconds, 24th place, after the eighth stage.

Margin of victory: 6 minutes, 44 seconds

Runners-up: Jan Ullrich, Joseba Beloki, Andrei Kivilev.

2002

The setup: Armstrong was the heavy favorite to become the fourth man to win four straight Tours, especially in a field that lacked some of cycling's stars.

Key stage: Trailing Igor Gonzalez de Galdeano by 27 seconds, Armstrong followed teammate Roberto Heras up the final climb of the 11th stage before pulling away. He ended the day with the yellow jersey.

Stages won: 4

AFTER WINNING STAGE 11 BY SEVEN SECONDS, LANCE ARMSTRONG IS BACK IN THE YELLOW JERSEY AS THE OVERALL LEADER OF THE 2002 TOUR.

TAYLOR JOHNSON/AUSTIN AMERICAN-STATESMAN

Biggest deficit: 34 seconds, eighth place after the seventh and eighth stages

Margin of victory: 7 minutes, 17 seconds

Runners-up: Joseba Beloki, Raimondas Rumsas, Santiago Botero.

2003

The setup: This Tour screamed history. It was the event's centennial and featured a route full of pomp and tradition. And Armstrong had a chance to become only the second man to win five Tours in a row.

Key stage: Armstrong entered the tortuous Stage 15 with only a 15-second lead of Jan Ullrich. Disaster struck when Armstrong fell to the ground. His competitors slowed to allow Armstrong catch up, and he then charged to a dramatic stage victory.

Stages won: 1

Biggest deficit: 2 minutes, 37 seconds after the seventh stage

Margin of victory: 1 minute, 1 second

Runners-up: Jan Ullrich, Alexandre Vinokourov, Tyler Hamilton.

LANCE ARMSTRONG SURVIVED
A HARROWING STAGE 15 IN 2003
AND VOLUNTEERS HELP STEADY
HIM AFTER CROSSING THE
FINISH LINE.

RODOLFO GONZALEZ/AUSTIN AMERICAN-STATESMAN

Tour de Lance
With victory at hand, Armstrong pads lead

S U Z A N N E   H A L L I B U R T O N
American-Statesman Staff

July 25, 1999

FUTUROSCOPE, France — Linda Armstrong was almost in tears Saturday afternoon as she gave into the emotions of seeing her only child, a near three-year cancer survivor, cement his status as one of the best athletes in the world. "I don't even have the words to describe this," she said as she desperately tried to hold back a sob. "We were facing death in the eye and to come back at this level . . . This proves that there is hope."

Moments earlier, Lance Armstrong, her 27-year-old son, had presented his mother, who had arrived here the night before, with two large bouquets, one of red flowers, signifying his victory Saturday in the Futuroscope time trial, and a yellow bunch of roses to commemorate his overall lead in the Tour de France.

A joyous Armstrong, who has grown stronger through the three-week long Tour, finished the 35.5-mile time trial in 1 hour, 8 minutes, 17 seconds. He was the last rider on the course, but he was so dominant that he passed his main competition, Fernando Escartin, despite the Spaniard's two-minute head start.

"To finish with a stage victory is just incredible," Armstrong said. "I really wanted to win this time trial badly. I didn't start with the same fire as in the Metz time trial, but I was really hungry to show the yellow jersey. I really suffered in the last 10 kilometers, and I knew it would come down to the best guy winning."

Added his mother, "His ride was awesome, but I never was sitting comfortable while he was out there. Every word out of my mouth was 'ride safe, ride safe, ride safe.'"

Armstrong had no problems riding fast and safe. He led at all four intermediate posts, averaging about 30 mph through the race. Most riders were begrudgingly conceding Saturday that Armstrong was by far the best

LINDA ARMSTRONG CELEBRATES WITH HER SON ON THE PODIUM AFTER LANCE WON THE 1999 TOUR DE FRANCE.

in this 2,400-mile race that ends today. The field will ride from Arpajon to downtown Paris, where the group will circle the 329-year-old Champs Elysees 10 times, with landmarks such as the Eiffel Tower, Grand Palais and the Arc de Triomphe serving as backdrops.

"Armstrong again confirmed that he was the strongest," said Alex Zulle, the Swiss rider who appeared to have won Saturday's time trial until Armstrong beat him by nine seconds. "I rode all out and took all kinds of risks throughout the three weeks, but couldn't beat the American. Again it was a hard day because of the wind and the pressure. But to lose by nine seconds only proves that, even without the crash in Gios (stage two), I couldn't have beaten Lance."

Armstrong picked up his fourth stage win. He won both Tour time trials and the short prologue that kicked off the event on July 3. He also won the first mountain stage in the French Alps on July 13.

Tyler Hamilton, Armstrong's U.S. Postal Service teammate, finished third in 1:09.52. Typically, the last time trial in the Tour has little effect on the overall standings. But Zulle was able to pass Escartin and take second place overall, but he still was 7:37 behind Armstrong. Escartin, who had been 6:15 behind Armstrong before Saturday, lost 4:11 during the stage that started and ended at Futuroscope, an amusement park about a three hours' drive south of Paris.

"I wanted to see what I had left after a three-week Tour, especially considering all the work I did for Lance," Hamilton said.

Armstrong and Hamilton helped tighten U.S. Postal's grasp as the Tour's best team, a feat in itself since the American group was one of the last to be included in the 20-team field. Armstrong's team received its invitation less than three weeks before the start of the Tour, while 16 of the teams, the ones designated as the world's best, knew they were riding to Paris back in January.

Saturday's stage was an emotional one for the smattering of Americans who were among the thousands of fans who stood 10 to 12 people deep in some places along the time-trial route. Linda Armstrong arrived in time from the Dallas suburb of Richardson to see her son claim victory. She was accompanied by Austin residents Danny and Charlotte Pounds, who live along the shores of Lake Austin near Armstrong's Mediterranean-style mansion.

"Lance's race was amazing," said Charlotte Pounds. "It's just a miracle."

A large Texas flag hung most of the afternoon from the back door of the U.S. Postal Service team van, which Armstrong used as a warm-up area. About 100 fans gathered beside the van more than an hour before Armstrong started the time trial. Included in that group were three members of the U.S. Disabled Cycling Team who had competed earlier in the day in a time trial of the European Open at Blois, about 100 miles from Futuroscope.

The trio wanted any kind of Armstrong souvenir. They were given the Postal team's signature blue caps.

"We made a point of making it down here," said David Conklin, a resident of LaCrosse, Wis., who suffered a spinal cord injury in a motorcycle accident. "This is so great for U.S. cycling. What Lance has overcome and his desire to compete is amazing."

Armstrong's immediate fan base will swell today when he is joined by his wife, Kristin, who has been to only a handful of stages because she is almost seven months pregnant with the couple's first child. Kristin Armstrong's mother, father and brother flew in from Minnesota to see the final stage.

About a half dozen of Armstrong's friends from Austin will also be present for basically a victory stroll through downtown Paris. To commemorate the final stage, Nike has furnished a special pair of yellow cycling shoes for Armstrong to wear. And Armstrong will use a new bicycle that has been painted navy blue and decorated with the insignia of the Lance Armstrong Foundation, which Armstrong created in November 1996, two months after he was diagnosed with an advanced form of testicular cancer, to promote awareness of the disease.

Sometime Saturday night, Linda Armstrong presented her son with gifts — a homemade loaf of banana bread, an "I love Daddy" bib for the newborn and a small travel-sized book filled with sayings and advice for new fathers.

"Lance has always wanted children," she said. "He's going to make a great dad."

HAVING GROWN STRONGER AT EVERY STAGE, LANCE ARMSTRONG DOMINATES THE INDIVIDUAL TIME TRIAL SPRINT OF THE 1999 TOUR.

"There's something special in winning in a sprint. To win in a sprint for me is much more intense than being alone."

LANCE ARMSTRONG

ARMSTRONG TAKES PARIS

Cyclist's triumph celebrated by fans as one of greatest comebacks in sport

SUZANNE HALLIBURTON AND JOHN MAHER
American-Statesman Staff

July 26, 1999

PARIS — The American was finally in Paris. After more than three weeks and 2,000 miles cycling across the French countryside and up and down its treacherous mountains, Austin's Lance Armstrong hit the cobblestone of Paris' boulevards. On Sunday, they were lined with thousands of fans chanting his name.

As the pack of cyclists approached the Eiffel Tower, riders of the U.S. Postal Service team surged to the front, then allowed Armstrong, their leader, to have a ceremonial ride up front. Under blue skies, he cruised to a remarkable victory in the 86th Tour de France.

"This is fantastic," Armstrong shouted, moments after he jumped off the winner's podium.

The 27-year-old cancer survivor, once the sport's boy wonder, had at last captured cycling's biggest race, and so much more. He won hearts. He won new respect. And he won a special place, not just in the history of cycling, but in all of sport.

The Tour, rocked by drug scandals last year, also emerged victorious.

"He is the best winner the Tour can imagine," Tour Director Jean Marie LeBlanc said through an interpreter. "The way Lance Armstrong overcame his perils, maybe he won the Tour because he fights more."

Before Armstrong's victory, Dr. Scott Shapiro, who had performed brain surgery on Armstrong less than three years ago, had said, "If he holds on and wins, it will be the greatest medical sports comeback in the history of the 20th century."

"I've been to hell and back," Armstrong said after winning. "I hope this sends a fantastic message to all the cancer patients around the world. We can return to what we were before — and be even better."

"It has to be one of the greatest stories in sports," said Davis Phinney, a former U.S. Olympic cyclist. "It's the biggest stage possible, and for him to put on that kind of bravura performance . . . The Tour de France is the most difficult endurance sport there is. It's like climbing Mount Everest every day with a time limit. It's not some made-up sport that five guys do. It's almost 100 years old. The best bike racers on the planet are there."

Phinney added: "It's raised my level of respect for him. I have appreciated his ability, but the true essence of a person, you don't find out that until you're tested outside of sport."

Lawrence Einhorn, one of the doctors who treated Armstrong in Indianapolis, said, "If Hollywood makes a movie of this, most people will leave the theater shaking their heads with incredulity."

Armstrong's great test began in October 1996. After he coughed up blood at his home in Austin, he learned that the swollen testicle he had been ignoring was cancerous. Worse, the cancer had spread. More than a dozen tumors, some the size of golf balls, grew in his lungs.

"He had a coin-flip possibility of living," said Craig Nichols, one of the doctors who treated Armstrong at Indiana University Medical Center in Indianapolis.

Armstrong put on a brave, determined face.

LANCE ARMSTRONG SHOULDERS THE AMERICAN FLAG FOR HIS VICTORY LAP ON THE AVENUE DES CHAMPS-ELYSÉES IN PARIS IN 1999.

RALPH BARRERA/AUSTIN AMERICAN-STATESMAN

"He's extremely tough and willful," Nichols said. "He assured me that he was going to beat it. He put the same focus on that as he does in cycling."

Armstrong has candidly acknowledged, however, that "regardless of the odds, I thought I was going to die."

For his treatment, he was strapped down for five days while cancer-fighting agents, including platinum, were dripped into his body.

"This type of therapy began in the 1970s," Nichols said. "Twenty years ago, his situation would have been fatal."

The agents that attacked the DNA of the cancer cells also attacked other rapidly dividing cells in his hair, fingernails and stomach lining.

"Chemotherapy in general is very debilitating," Nichols said. "There's vomiting, dehydration and weight loss."

The treatment is such a shock to the system that three weeks must pass before another five-day round of treatment can begin.

For Armstrong's treatment, one modification was made. Drugs that were harder on bone marrow but less damaging to the lungs — cisplatin and etoposide — were tried in the hope that if he lived, he might be able to return to cycling.

Armstrong endured four such treatments. And when he could, he continued to cycle, even if it was more to divert his mind than to train.

"He had women in his neighborhood who could beat him. He was at one-tenth of his capacity," Nichols said.

But after he was given his doctors' permission, Armstrong went to the Human Performance Laboratory at the University of Texas.

"He was convinced he'd done some damage to his lungs," said Eddie Coyle, head of the lab.

After years of testing Armstrong, Coyle had reams of data on him. He studied it and made a prediction about what Armstrong's performance would be doing his moderate workouts of 50-mile rides at 160 heartbeats per minute. When Armstrong was tested, he almost matched those numbers, meaning that his lowered performance was due not to permanent damage, but to a lack of training.

Almost immediately, he began pushing harder. Although he had some encouraging results in 1998, few expected him to dominate a race that only one other American, Greg LeMond, had won.

Until Sunday, LeMond's story was the most remarkable of the Tour. LeMond won in 1986 and then suffered a near-fatal hunting accident in 1987. He came back to win the Tour in 1989 and 1990.

Athletes in other sports have made dramatic comebacks as well. Several baseball players, including John Kruk, Eric Davis, Darryl Strawberry and Brett Butler, have come back after bouts with cancer. Boxer George Foreman beat Father Time, claiming a heavyweight title 20 years after being stunned by Muhammad Ali. Golfer Ben Hogan won the 1950 U.S. Open a little more than a year after his Cadillac lost a head-on collision with a bus. Basketball star Magic Johnson returned to the Los Angeles Lakers in the 1995-96 season after sitting out four years after testing positive for the human immunodeficiency virus.

Armstrong, however, not only came back after cancer, but he reached a new level of excellence.

And he rode for more than just his own glory.

He started the Lance Armstrong Foundation two years ago. It raises money to fight cancer, and he has become a spokesman and role model.

"My dad relates to him. He's had cancer and was given a 10 percent chance of living," Phinney said of his father, Damon. "That was 12 years ago. But I don't think he ever thought he was doing anything other than forestalling the inevitable. But now he's seen what Lance has done. He's out there riding a bike. He believes, and that can be powerful. Lance has that power to wield, and he's wielding it like a Jedi knight."

On Sunday, Armstrong was closely followed by a horde of paparazzi on motorcycles as he rode his victory lap along the Champs-Elysees. American tourists waved flags.

"It's been so strange to be an American in Paris this week," said Atlanta resident Michael Colwell. "Just last week, we heard reports that John F. Kennedy Jr. had died, and it was so sad to lose someone like him. Then, in the same week, we have somebody like Lance Armstrong do this. It's incredible. I heard a guy talking, and he said that Lance winning is the best thing that can happen to cancer patients because of all the money that will be raised because of him for cancer research."

Dr. Steven Wolf, president of the Lance Armstrong Foundation, said: "When I first met Lance, I was concerned about whether he was going to live or die from his illness. What a tribute to a special man. Lance was a great patient; he has the heart of a lion. He got the chance to live, and he took it, and it's such a wonderful thing because with Lance winning the Tour, our work is now just beginning."

> *"He believes, and that can be powerful. Lance has that power to wield, and he's wielding it like a Jedi knight."*
>
> *DAVIS PHINNEY, FORMER OLYMPIC CYCLIST*

**THE U.S. POSTAL SERVICE TEAM PROTECTS
LANCE ARMSTRONG FROM THE FRONT AS THEY
RIDE TO THE FINISH LINE OF THE FINAL STAGE
OF THE 1999 RACE.**

RALPH BARRERA/AUSTIN AMERICAN-STATESMAN

LANCE ARMSTRONG ANNOUNCES, IN 1998 THAT THE
LANCE ARMSTRONG FOUNDATION WILL AWARD TWO
RESEARCH GRANTS WORTH MORE THAN A QUAR-
TER OF A MILLION DOLLARS TO THE UNIVERSITY
OF TEXAS M.D. ANDERSON CANCER CENTER IN
HOUSTON AND VANDERBILT UNIVERSITY MEDICAL
CENTER IN NASHVILLE, TENNESSEE.

PHONES JINGLING AFTER TOUR VICTORY

Lance Armstrong Foundation for cancer research gets boost

GARY ESTWICK
American-Statesman Staff

July 27, 1999

The phone lines at the Lance Armstrong Foundation haven't stopped ringing since Austin cyclist Lance Armstrong started the Tour de France on July 3 and finished it as champion on Sunday in Paris. "It's been crazy over here all morning," said foundation director Karl Haussman, while receiving another call as one of the foundation's three-member staff. "But that's a good thing, that's an awesome thing. The beauty of all that is happening is that we're getting our name out.

"It's all about exposure for the foundation spreading our message. Those are all great things for the foundation."

Armstrong, 27, overcame his own life-threatening bout with testicular cancer after being diagnosed in 1996. He did not compete in 1997, taking the year off to recuperate from extensive chemotherapy. He raced a limited schedule last year and on Sunday showed the world his comeback was complete by becoming the first American to win the Tour since Greg LeMond in 1990.

"Lance really sees this as more than a victory on the Tour and for the foundation but also the cancer community," Haussman said. "Anyone surviving cancer, this is a victory for them, too. You can come back from the lowest of the lows.

"You have to take the opportunity and fight for your life."

Foundation board member Scott Gidley said people can relate to Armstrong's never-say-die attitude. "I

> *"Lance really sees this as more than a victory on the Tour and for the foundation but also the cancer community."*
>
> KARL HAUSSMAN, FOUNDATION DIRECTOR

think people with diseases and disabilities can look to him and the way he attacked the disease."

Armstrong's win has benefited the foundation, a non-profit agency founded in 1997 to support patients and survivors of urological cancer. Foundation officials said the organization has raised approximately $40,000 over the last two months, totaling roughly $1,000,000 in donations since its inception. In 1998, total donations were approximately $400,000.

The foundation supports cancer patients and survivors through education, awareness and research.

The foundation's Web site has also been a source of information, receiving about 50,000 visitors since May. Because of limited television coverage, the Internet also was a favorite place for Tour fans to find race results.

Armstrong's success has meant corporate sponsorships for the foundation. Nike Inc., a regular LAF supporter, recently donated $25,000. Haussman said the foundation hopes Armstrong's success will mean more local and national corporate partnerships.

Dawn Leonetti, ACG (all-conditions gear) communication manager of Nike, said the donation was designed to motivate other companies and individuals to do the same.

"We really see Lance as the epitome of the 'just do it' athlete that Nike has," Leonetti said. "We think Lance transcends to people around the world as a symbol for cancer survivors and people everywhere."

Since 1997, Nike has donated $55,000 to the LAF and its primarily fund-raiser, the Ride for the Roses.

Haussman said the foundation hopes to get more local and national corporate partnerships.

The foundation, composed of business and medical leaders throughout the country, funds clinical research, educational projects and fellowships for urological cancer. Haussman said before the LAF was formed in 1996, little medical research was done for testicular cancer. Haussman added the LAF plans to address additional forms of cancer next year.

HOW TO CONTRIBUTE

The Lance Armstrong Foundation accepts donations that fund research projects, awareness campaigns and educational programs related to fighting and preventing cancer. The foundation also sponsors the annual Ride for the Roses Weekend in Austin, which raises hundreds of thousands of dollars.

To contribute, write, call, or visit the foundation's website:

Lance Armstrong Foundation
P.O. Box 161150
Austin, TX 78716-1150
1-800-496-4402
www. laf.org

"We think Lance transcends to people around the world as a symbol for cancer survivors and people everywhere."

DAWN LEONETTI, NIKE

STUDENTS AT HILL ELEMENTARY
SCHOOL, WHO WERE INVOLVED
WITH FUNDRAISING FOR THE LANCE
ARMSTRONG FOUNDATION, WAIT
IN LINE TO GET THEIR SHIRTS
AND POSTERS AUTOGRAPHED BY
ARMSTRONG.

FANS FROM AUSTIN, TEXAS—CHRIS
KISKE (LEFT), SOFIA KISKE (CENTER)
AND CAROLYN KERBY (RIGHT)—SHOW
THEIR SUPPORT FOR HOMETOWN HERO
LANCE ARMSTRONG.

TAYLOR JOHNSON/AUSTIN AMERICAN-STATESMAN

"Yellow wakes me up in the morning. Yellow gets me on the bike every day. Yellow has taught me the true meaning of sacrifice. Yellow makes me suffer. Yellow is the reason I'm here."

LANCE ARMSTRONG

A DAY WITH LANCE ARMSTRONG

DON TATE
American-Statesman staff

July 4, 2000

My assignment: To report on what a day at the Tour de France is like for Lance Armstrong. Now, I'm just the graphics reporter, so my assignment didn't involve traveling to Paris and hangin' with Lance. I didn't get to question him over coffee and power bars. He did return my e-mail, and this is some of what he shared with me.

Morning
• 9 a.m. Lance is up and ready to start his day with breakfast. Bet you were thinking Wheaties, right? No, it's Kellogg's Mueslix cereal.

• After a chiropractic adjustment for his back, Lance begins a regimen of stretching exercises and prepares for the day's stage.

Afternoon
• 1-5 p.m. Pedal, pedal, pedal ... Lunch is eaten on the bike during the race sometime after the first hour. Munching continues until about an hour before the end of the day's race. During that time, Lance consumes lots of simple sugars in the form of high-energy bars, cookies and power gels.

Evening
• Immediately following the day's race he's eating complex carbohydrates like potatoes and pasta.

• A massage is in order after 100-plus miles of hill climbing. There are four massage therapists for the nine riders on the U.S. Postal Service team.

• A dinner of pasta and a meat is prepared for late evening. Risotto, an Italian dish of rice or pasta with meat, is one of his favorites.

• The remainder of his evening is spent relaxing in his hotel room or granting interviews with the press.

• 10 p.m. It's bedtime. He needs at least nine hours of sleep to be rested for the next day's race.

Vitals:
• Resting heart rate: 32-34 beats per minute

• Maximum heart rate: 201

• Heart rate during endurance rides: (four to six hours) 124-128

• Height: 5 feet, 11 inches

• Weight: 160 pounds

• Body fat: 3 percent

LANCE ARMSTRONG AND MECHANIC DAVE LATTIERI MAKE ADJUSTMENTS TO HIS SEAT BEFORE A TRAINING RIDE.

TAYLOR JOHNSON/AUSTIN AMERICAN-STATESMAN

Today, Lance Armstrong should roll into Paris and claim the Tour de France for the second year in a row, further securing his status as an American hero.

TOUR NEARS END AS ARMSTRONG READIES THE CHAMPAGNE

SUZANNE HALLIBURTON
American-Statesman Staff

July 23, 2000

TROYES, FRANCE—He has maintained a substantial lead in the Tour de France since that first day he strode to the podium and donned the yellow jersey, after his monumental effort up the Hautacam almost two weeks ago. But Lance Armstrong, publicly, would never let his comments stray too far from the next Tour stage.

On Saturday, about an hour after Armstrong completed stage 20, a 157.8-mile trip between Belfort and Troyes, the Tour peloton, or main pack, got to within 120 miles of the finish line on the cobblestoned Champs Elysees.

So it was time to talk about Paris. It seemed appropriate that the Tour made a stop in champagne country Saturday, because, barring some catastrophic event, the Armstrong family will soon be popping corks to celebrate his repeat victory.

"OK, we'll be in Paris tomorrow," Armstrong said Saturday. "But I still have to be careful. The stage still counts. It's still an official stage.

"I still won't be convinced about my victory until I get there. I'll stay around the team and stay out of trouble until then."

This morning, the 128 riders who remain for the final stage of this three-week event will board the legendary Orient Express and travel to Paris. They will start today at the Eiffel Tower at 2 p.m. local time, 7 a.m. in Austin. Just after 4:30 p.m. in Paris, Armstrong should be standing on the podium ready to celebrate what he termed was a more physically exhausting championship than last year's.

He owns a lead of 6 minutes, 2 seconds over Jan Ullrich. Typically, little if any time is made up in the last day of the Tour, with a smattering of sprinters trying to win the stage and the rest of the peloton riding casually to celebrate getting to the end after more than 2,200 miles of riding.

Despite the imminency of the Tour's final day, Saturday was a legitimate stage, one that went through relatively flat terrain in the eastern stretches of France. It was the sprinters who dominated the penultimate stage, with Eric Zabel, the most consistent of them all, taking the win over Robbie McEwen.

Aside from awarding the yellow jersey each day, Tour sponsors also present a green one to the best sprinter of the bunch, with points awarded daily. Today, Zabel will get his fifth green jersey in a row.

But the 30-year-old German, despite his overall excellence in the sprints, hadn't won a stage since 1997. He had most of his Deutsche Telekom team working for him late in the stage Saturday, with two riders taking

"No one automatically gives you respect just because you show up. You have to earn it." — LANCE ARMSTRONG

**LANCE ARMSTRONG RIDES WITH THE
PELOTON DURING STAGE 21 IN PARIS IN 2000.**

TAYLOR JOHNSON/AUSTIN AMERICAN-STATESMAN

turns at the front of the peloton, wildly churning toward the finish while allowing Zabel to draft behind them and preserve energy.

With less than 500 meters to go, the last Telekom protector peeled away from the pack, allowing Zabel to take over. With George Hincapie of U.S. Postal and U.S. Pro champion Fred Rodriguez giving chase, Zabel leaned forward and threw out his arms, nosing past McEwen and Jeroen Blijlevens for the victory. A photo finish showed a difference of about two inches between the three riders.

"I give a big thanks to my team," Zabel said. "They did good work. Three years is too long to wait. It's hard to imagine that I won."

One hundred and one of the riders, including Armstrong, finished with the same winning time as Zabel — 6 hours, 14 minutes and 13 seconds. Armstrong, whose team rode at the front of the peloton to protect their leader for much of the afternoon, finished 27th. Ullrich was 24th.

Hincapie was ninth and Rodriguez was 15th.

Johan Bruynee, the U.S. Postal director sportif, had given orders to protect Armstrong at all cost. That was an easy assignment, given that Team Postal was the only squad with its full allotment of nine riders still in the Tour.

The Nike Swift Spin Suit Lance Armstrong wears is nearly 22 percent lighter than a standard Tour-issue short-sleeve time trial suit, and up to 35 percent lighter than a standard jersey and bib shorts. Design highlights include:

- Lightweight power net mesh is placed along the side of the torso and down the spine. Nike Sports Research Lab testing has shown these areas to be the most effective locations for cooling. Power mesh placed along the side of the thighs balances cooling with typical levels of leg compression;

- Waist expansion panel stretches to improve comfort while standing yet returns to provide a close fit when in the riding position;

- Eyelet mesh on the front chest balances cooling with surface turbulence concerns;

- Finely tuned textured fabric on the arms and legs generates surface turbulence in these zones where airflow typically detaches from the body.

LANCE AND LUKE ARMSTRONG WALK AWAY FROM THE WINNER'S PODIUM IN PARIS AFTER ARMSTRONG WON HIS SECOND TOUR DE FRANCE.

MAKING OF THE MAN

*When other champions peer into Armstrong's eyes, they
see that incredible drive, that amazing willpower*

KIRK BOHLS
American-Statesman Staff

July 24, 2000

It's in his eyes. Lance Armstrong has the look of a champion. The look of a man so possessed of dream, so obsessed with what it is he wants to accomplish, that the heart ignores fatigue and exhaustion and wills the body to push itself beyond the normal bounds.

Had she not known the undeniable outcome of the Tour de France, a grueling, three-week endurance contest, Jill Sterkel still would have recognized the fierce, unrelenting spirit that pushed Armstrong to ride down the Champs-Elysees as champion once more.

Those pale blue eyes tell it all. Sterkel, a four-time Olympic swimmer and gold medalist, sees the embodiment of that unparalleled inner drive in Armstrong's steely gaze that never has wavered.

"Here's a guy who's been at the bottom of life," said Sterkel, the University of Texas women's swimming coach who won two gold and two bronze medals in Olympics spanning 12 years. "You can see the determination and the focus in his eyes. I wish I could suck it out of him and put it in some other people. He's figured it out. If you want to be great, look at Lance Armstrong."

For more than half of the 21-stage event, the other riders were looking at him — from behind.

In wiping away the field as he did under the most severe conditions imaginable, where the mountain descents are every bit as dangerous as the climbs, Armstrong established himself as one of the elite athletes in American sports history. In addition, he reaffirmed himself in the pantheon of Austin heroes such as Ricky Williams, Darrell Royal, Ben Crenshaw and Jody Conradt.

"Lance is such a compelling story, it's captivated all of us," said Conradt, the Basketball Hall of Fame coach from the University of Texas who has kept tabs on Armstrong's progress while recruiting at Amateur Athletic Union tournaments in Tennessee. "In Austin, having experienced the support for women's sports, we know it's a city that embraces some non-traditional sports. Of course, you have to be No. 1 or better."

Armstrong had already won the respect and admiration of sports fans worldwide, but by repeating in such spectacular fashion he further esconces himself in the lore of American sports.

"Lance Armstrong represents everything that is right," Texas football coach Mack Brown said. "He has shown unparalleled courage and has the talent to be the best in the world at what he does, and he does it with class. Most of all, he's a nice guy who believed that he could do anything and was willing to work hard enough to make that happen. That defines a champion."

> *"I think it's the most incredible American sports story I've seen in years, maybe ever. It's a blessing from the good Lord."*
>
> — *EARL CAMPBELL, FORMER UNIVERSITY OF TEXAS HEISMAN TROPHY WINNER*

Armstrong, a lanky 28-year-old Texan whose lean physique carries 3 percent body fat, shocked the world a year ago when he won his first Tour de France in impos-

EVEN AS A YOUNG RACER, SHOWN HERE IN
1991 NEAR HIS HOME IN AUSTIN, TEXAS,
LANCE ARMSTRONG EXHIBITED THE QUALITIES
AND DRIVE OF A CHAMPION.

LANCE ARMSTRONG AND THE U.S. POSTAL
SERVICE TEAM RIDE INTO PARIS TO WIN
THE 1999 TOUR DE FRANCE.

RALPH BARRERA/AUSTIN AMERICAN-STATESMAN

ing fashion. The win came after he was diagnosed with testicular cancer in October 1996, and he had taken a full year off from competitive riding.

Winning the Tour again stamps him as one of the greatest cyclists ever.

Sterkel can relate. She brought home a gold medal from the Montreal Olympic Games in 1976 at the tender age of 15 after swimming a leg of the 400-meter relay team. Eight years later she swam on the same winning relay squad in the Olympic Games at Los Angeles.

"I think it gets harder the second time," Sterkel said. "The first time I had no clue what I was doing."

As an older and more mature athlete, Sterkel said she learned how to balance the pressures of performing with the rush of competing. She learned how to internalize the pressure.

So, too, did Keith Moreland as a catcher and designated hitter for the world-champion Philadelphia Phillies in 1980. The former All-America third baseman for the Texas Longhorns reached the pinnacle of his 12-year major-league baseball career in just his third season as the Mike Schmidt-led Phillies beat the Kansas City Royals in the World Series.

Although those same Phils jumped to a five-game lead in the summer of 1981, a strike interrupted their defense of the crown, and they didn't survive the truncated season with split-season champions.

"Everybody in the world is shooting at you," Moreland said. "You could tell the difference. We had basically the same club, but we'd go in every city where when they introduced the starting lineups and said, 'Now for the visiting world-champion Phillies . . .'"

Conradt, the all-time winningest women's basketball coach, captured a national championship in 1986 with a perfect record and has been to only one Final Four since 1986. "You do it the first time, you think it's going to happen again," she said. "You don't realize how difficult it'll be."

Armstrong repeated without so much as a bump.

Instead of shrinking under the weight of the expectations, he stunned the competition and the sports world by taking the lead at the 10th stage and never looking back.

"A bike ride. Yes, that's it! A simple bike ride. It's what I love to do and most days I can't believe they pay me to do it. A day is not the same without it . . ."
LANCE ARMSTRONG'S RESPONSE WHEN ASKED
"WHAT IS YOUR FAVORITE THING?"

In 1999, Armstrong was accepted as a champion of champions by everyone except the French in what is his adopted second homeland.

Critics harped on his failure to speak in French at his press conferences. Others absurdly protested that he was using performance-enhancing drugs, although we're still waiting on the rush of cyclists to take chemotherapy before the Tour. Some decried the lack of competition with so many top riders absent, as if that could be blamed on Armstrong.

Even with his miraculous ride through the French countryside in 1999, this year was going to be different.

The field was better. The course more difficult. The expectations bigger. Instead of being considered a bigger novelty than rain clouds over Austin, Armstrong was the focus, the target.

Recognized as the favorite to become the first American to repeat as Tour champion since three-time winner Greg LeMond, Armstrong backed off some after a crash into a wall at the Col du Solour when he hit a rock. He emerged in late June as a fresh, supremely confident rider.

He bided his time in the flat lands of western France where the sprinters were dominant and then gutted it up to take a commanding lead while racing up the side of Mount Venoux that looked like the final wave of *The Perfect Storm.*

Under the weight of such intense anticipation, Armstrong not only persevered in this year's race, he raised the level of his cycling. As Campbell noted, Armstrong adjusted his training after his bout with cancer and remained implanted on his bike.

"If not for his cancer, he wouldn't have changed his training," Campbell said. "He learned standing up burns more energy. If you sit down, you're stronger. Maybe it was meant to be."

Like a true champion, Armstrong proved he was no one-year wonder. This was no comeback, just confirmation that Armstrong is among the greatest cyclists of all-time.

"This is my body. And I can do whatever I want to it. I can push it. Study it. Tweak it. Listen to it. Everybody wants to know what I'm on. What am I on? I'm on my bike busting my ass six hours a day. What are you on?"

— *LANCE ARMSTRONG*

Heart is so hard to define, but all will agree it is the one intangible that separates the contenders from the pretenders. No one questions the mental resolve of Armstrong, who not only repeated but improved on his 1999 performance against even greater odds.

Of course, his has been a career that's not about limits but possibilities, not about risks, but rewards.

While some might have written off his 1999 championship as a fluke, one of those bizarre sports occurrences that no one can explain like a Bud Adams team in the Super Bowl, a Northwestern team in the Rose Bowl or a Buster Douglas upset of Mike Tyson, no one can dismiss two Tour de France titles in a row. Not this time when Armstrong had to fight off the charges of previous winners Marco Pantani and Jan Ullrich and other former world champions such as Lauren Jalabert.

"Lance Armstrong's achievements in the Tour de France are inspiring, and reflect his phenomenal drive for success," said computer company mogul Michael Dell, who knows something about hard drive.

At the other end of the spectrum, Austin music giant Willie Nelson says, "I have all the admiration and respect in the world for Lance Armstrong. He is a winner in every way."

So where does Lance go from here besides Jay Leno's couch? Does he set his sights on three Tour de France victories or four or take aim at the five titles of Jacques Anquetil, Bernard Hinault, Eddy Merckx and Miguel Indurain? Does he retire at the top of his game and raise his family? Has he had his fill of this torturous profession?

Armstrong has already shown he's the Tiger Woods of cycling, the Mark McGwire of the mountains. No cyclist has the raw power he packs on a lithe, 5-foot-11-inch, 160-pound frame.

While other riders, Pantani among them, dropped by the wayside, victim of injury or illness, Armstrong only got stronger. Few have the fiery resolve of this unquestionably supremely conditioned athlete.

Sterkel thinks of Armstrong's accomplishment and shakes her head in disbelief.

She can identify with Armstrong better than most. Her father, Jim Sterkel, a former basketball player at Southern California, fought lymphoma for five years and once was considered cancer-free before succumbing to the disease at age 63 in 1997.

"I saw my dad at the bottom of the bottom," Sterkel said. "It's a sight I'll never forget. It must have been the same for Lance. He was basically a goner. But Lance has that inner drive, and if you add the fuel, no one can beat him."

For two years riding, no one has.

"I rode, and I rode, and I rode. I rode like I had never ridden, punishing my body up and down every hill I could find . . . . I rode when no one else would ride, not even my teammates . . ."
— LANCE ARMSTRONG ON TRAINING
FOR THE TOUR DE FRANCE

ABOVE: LANCE ARMSTRONG SALUTES THE FLAG AS HE LISTENS TO THE NATIONAL ANTHEM AFTER WINNING HIS THIRD CONSECUTIVE TOUR.

OPPOSITE: ARMSTRONG (LEFT) FINISHED THE THIRD STAGE IN 10TH PLACE AND JAN ULLRICH (RIGHT) FINISHED 13TH, BUT BOTH ARE IN THE TOP 10 OVERALL IN 2000.

**LANCE ARMSTRONG FACED
ADVERSITY IN MANY FORMS
AND CAME OUT OF IT
STRONGER THAN EVER.**

TAYLOR JOHNSON/AUSTIN AMERICAN-STATESMAN

LANCE 3

Armstrong's third straight win puts him among elite

SUZANNE HALLIBURTON
American-Statesman Staff

July 30, 2001

PARIS — Riding into this European capital with strength and poise, Lance Armstrong won his third consecutive Tour de France on Sunday, rising to the exclusive tier of world athletes who dominate their sports for years. On a sweltering midsummer afternoon, Armstrong streamed into the city with 143 other cyclists, finishing the grueling three-week, 2,151-mile route through France and Belgium with more than a 6-minute advantage over his closest competitor, Jan Ullrich of Germany.

In front of crowds estimated at more than 100,000, Armstrong and fellow members of the U.S. Postal Service team took up American and Texas flags and celebrated with victory laps over the cobblestones of this city's most famed boulevard, the Champs Elysees.

With this victory, the Austinite becomes the most dominant U.S. cyclist ever and joins a group of only eight cyclists to ever win three or more tours.

Before Sunday, only four men had won at least three Tours in a row: Louison Bobet of France (1953-55), Jacques Anquetil of France (1961-64), Eddy Merckx of Belgium (1969-72) and Miguel Indurain of Spain (1991-95).

"I put Lance in the top five athletes in the world in any sport," said American cyclist Davis Phinney, the 1984 Olympic bronze medalist who won stages in the Tour in 1986 and 1987. "By the time he's done, he'll reach legendary status. He'll sit on that top, top shelf."

"Lance has entered that inner circle," Armstrong's personal coach, Chris Carmichael, said Sunday. "I told

"I don't need to ride for the money, I do it because I love it and I would happily ride for nothing. I will be riding a bike in 10 years' time because I feel better when I do exercise and I want to enjoy true good health."

LANCE ARMSTRONG

him in 1991 he'd win the Tour de France. I didn't know about three."

When Armstrong took the leader's yellow jersey in Stage 13, international cycling reporters began wondering not whether he would win the Tour, but about how many Tours he would win.

He had just come back from a 35-minute deficit, greater than any rider had overcome in more than 50 years. He was clawing his way into the lead in the mountains, and the climbers were struggling unsuccessfully to stay with him. Could Armstrong do the unthinkable? Could the Texan win six in a row?

The record is five. It is co-owned by the greatest names in cycling: Merckx, Indurain, Anquetil and Bernard Hinault of France.

"I think he can win six, but it depends on the quality of the opposition," says Jeremy Whittle, editor of London-based *Procycling* magazine. "To prove himself again, he needs fresh competition. He needs somebody to come along and challenge him. He's so determined and focused, you could see him winning five. If he won five, I can see him trying to win six."

Armstrong declined to talk about any of this speculation on Sunday. He said he will return next year to defend his title with a fourth championship. Other than that, he will not say how long he will race. His contract with Postal runs through 2004.

"As long as the passion stays, I'll be around, at least for four years," he said. "But if the passion starts to fade . . . I don't want to be one of those athletes who tries to rediscover their passion, only to see it never come back, and they can't go out on top."

Merckx, considered by many to be the best who ever rode, won his five titles in 1969-72 and 1974. His quest for a sixth title in 1975 ended with him finishing second to Bernard Thevenet. Merckx was so dominating that he earned the nickname "Cannibal," because he devoured all his competition.

He sees Armstrong continuing his Tour domination.

"As well as being extremely talented, Lance has great dedication, which makes him the favorite for still a few years to come," said Merckx, who serves as an adviser to Armstrong and has been to Austin twice to support Armstrong's foundation, which helps people manage and survive cancer.

"Lance has the uncanny ability to prepare the race in its utmost detail (and) has a team that fully backs him."

He also has the ability to win when the odds are against him.

His first Tour victory in 1999 proved that. Less than three years before, doctors had diagnosed him with advanced testicular cancer and had given him a less than 50-50 chance to overcome the disease.

With an effort that captured the imaginations of people worldwide, Armstrong not only came back from the cancer, but he came back to win the 1999 Tour, beating Switzerland's Alex Zulle by 7 minutes, 37 seconds, the third-largest margin of victory that decade.

In 2000, Armstrong successfully defended his championship, overwhelming a stronger field that included Ullrich, the 1997 champion, and Italy's Marco Pantani, the 1998 victor. Armstrong's margin over second-place Ullrich was 6:02.

After the 2000 Tour, Ullrich won gold and silver medals at the Olympics in Sydney. He is considered the most physically gifted cyclist in the world, and he trained harder than ever for this Tour. Still, he fell even further behind Armstrong this month, losing by 6:44. It was his fourth runner-up finish in five years.

"I can't try to be like him," Ullrich said of Armstrong. "I have to do things my way. I am now very motivated for next year. He's a great rider and was the strongest this year."

As in previous years, Armstrong was dogged by questions of whether he can be as good as he has been without the use of banned performance-enhancing substances.

While winning four stages, Armstrong was being asked about his relationship with Michele Ferrari, an Italian doctor who is set to stand trial in Bologna, Italy in September on doping charges. When the Tour kicked off in Dunkirk on July 7, Armstrong acknowledged that he had used Ferrari as a consultant on altitude training and nutrition. On July 23, when the Tour took a day off, Armstrong spent much of a 70-minute news conference answering questions about drugs.

Italian prosecutors began investigating Ferrari in 1998. More than 20 leading cyclists, including star sprinter Mario Cipollini, Abraham Olano and Eddy Merckx's son Axel were listed as "offended parties" or victims in the case against Ferrari. He is charged with administering such performance-enhancing drugs as adrenaline, testosterone, human growth hormones and anabolic steroids.

LANCE ARMSTRONG AND THE U.S. POSTAL TEAM FINISH THE 2000 TOUR'S STAGE 5 FOURTH PLACE ON A COLD, RAINY DAY IN NORTHERN FRANCE. AT FAR RIGHT IS TYLER HAMILTON AND JUST BEHIND ARMSTRONG IS HUGO PENA. GEORGE HINCAPIE IS FAR LEFT AND IN THE BACKGROUND IS CHRISTIAN VANDEVELDE. ARMSTRONG MOVED TO 15TH PLACE OVERALL.

TAYLOR JOHNSON/AUSTIN AMERICAN-STATESMAN

Ferrari is set to stand trial in September.

Greg LeMond, the American cyclist who won Tours in 1987 and 1989-90, was unavailable to the U.S. media in the past week. However, comments he made about Armstrong appeared in a story in the *Sunday Times* in London.

"When Lance won the prologue to the 1999 Tour, I was close to tears," LeMond was quoted as saying. "When I heard he was working with Michele Ferrari, I was devastated. If Lance is clean, it is the greatest comeback in the history of sport. If he isn't, it would be the greatest fraud."

LeMond told the paper that "in light of Lance's relationship with Ferrari, I just don't want to comment on this year's Tour."

Armstrong, with 42 drug tests, has been screened more than any other cyclist in the past three Tours. He has never tested positive for a banned substance, and he has repeatedly denied that he uses any drugs.

He said the drug speculation, like his competition with Ullrich, motivated him throughout the Tour.

"A little heated press conference on the rest day was probably all I needed," he said. "I like the competition."

"Cancer taught me a plan for more purposeful living. It taught me that pain has a reason, and that sometimes the experience of losing things has its own value in the scheme of life."

LANCE ARMSTRONG

ARMSTRONG TAKES HIS VICTORY LAP

Everybody wants a piece of the three-time Tour de France champ

SUZANNE HALLIBURTON
American-Statesman Staff

July 31, 2001

PARIS — On Sunday along the Champs Elysees, Paris' historic avenue, three-time defending champion Lance Armstrong took in all the chaotic madness that makes the Tour de France one of the biggest sporting spectacles in the world. Now, Armstrong will tell the United States how he feels about his victory. He will fly to New York today for a whirlwind trip of parties and media interviews.

Bill Stapleton, Armstrong's agent, said Armstrong will appear on a number of television shows. On Wednesday, Armstrong will make an appearance on CBS' *The Late Show with David Letterman*. On Thursday, Armstrong is scheduled to appear on NBC's *The Today Show*, ABC's *Good Morning America* and NBC's *Live with Regis and Kelly*. He also is expected to appear on PBS' *The Charlie Rose Show* and MSNBC's *Hardball*.

Sandwiched in between the interviews will be a baseball game. On Wednesday, Armstrong will throw out the first pitch for the New York Yankees' home game against the Texas Rangers. Thursday, the U.S. Postal Service will throw a party in New York to celebrate Armstrong's Tour achievement. Armstrong rides for the U.S. Postal Service team.

There is a possibility Armstrong will briefly return to Austin by week's end. The Lance Armstrong Foundation and the Greater Austin Sports Foundation said that as of Monday, there were no celebration plans scheduled in the city.

Armstrong still has some racing to do. There is a 50-50 chance he will ride in next month's Tour of Spain, where Postal teammate Roberto Heras is the defending champion. Armstrong has said he wants to ride in the event to help Heras defend his championship.

If he does ride in Spain, Armstrong will return to Austin at the end of September and remain in Texas for the off-season.

WITH THE TEXAS FLAG WAVING, LANCE ARMSTRONG AND HIS TEAMMATES TAKE THEIR VICTORY LAP IN 2001.

TAYLOR JOHNSON/AUSTIN AMERICAN-STATESMAN

THE PELOTON PASSES
THROUGH SUNFLOWER
COUNTRY DURING STAGE 15 OF
THE 2001 TOUR DE FRANCE.
LANCE ARMSTRONG IS JUST
VISIBLE IN THE YELLOW JER-
SEY LEFT OF CENTER.

> *"If you ever get a second chance in life for something, you've got to go all the way."*
>
> *LANCE ARMSTRONG*

LANCE ARMSTRONG IS ON THE VERGE OF JOINING CYCLING'S LEGENDS, AND EVEN GAINING GRUDGING ACCEPTANCE IN FRANCE

SUZANNE HALLIBURTON
American-Statesman Staff

July 4, 2002

Since last July, when Lance Armstrong won his third consecutive Tour de France, his fame in the United States has grown considerably. New York Mayor Rudy Giuliani invited Armstrong to take a helicopter tour of the World Trade Center ruins. He has dined with President Bush and former President Clinton. Burns Sports and Celebrities Inc., which publishes a yearly survey of business and advertising executives, said Armstrong is the third most-popular product endorser in all of sports, after Tiger Woods and Michael Jordan.

Armstrong, an Austin resident, is favored to win this year's Tour, which begins Saturday in Luxembourg when 189 riders from 21 teams compete against the clock in a time trial. If he wins the three-week race, he would become only the fourth cyclist ever to win four consecutive titles.

Yet only now — and begrudgingly — is the European cycling establishment beginning to accept Armstrong as one of the sport's all-time greatest.

"It's the French who get uptight because he keeps winning their race, and they are particularly conservative," said Jeremy Whittle, editor of London-based Procycling magazine. "The French, in particular, don't really like change. The Tour is seen as a cornerstone of continuing and unchanging French cultural life, like cheese, sunflowers, wine and pate. The French don't want the Tour turned into an American corporate jamboree."

More than 15 million fans are expected to line the 2,035-mile route over the next three weeks.

After Saturday's time trial, the race darts briefly into Germany before it heads back to France, going in a counterclockwise loop through champagne and Beaujolais vineyards, past 1,000-year-old churches and chateaus, from the shores of the Brittany coast south to

LANCE ARMSTRONG HAS MADE HIMSELF A GIANT IN THE SPORT OF CYCLING AND CONSISTENTLY DRAWS NEW SUPPORTERS WORLDWIDE.

TAYLOR JOHNSON/AUSTIN AMERICAN-STATESMAN

the Pyrenees straddling the French-Spanish border.

The race makes a late push through the towering Alps near Switzerland, then the riders wearily turn toward the finish line in Paris on July 28.

Against a backdrop of the Arc de Triomphe and the Eiffel Tower, a half-million fans will celebrate the man wearing the yellow jersey, which the Tour champion wears.

For the past three years, Armstrong has worn yellow as he waved both the U.S. and Texas flags on his victory stroll on the Champs Elysees. With a fourth straight victory, Armstrong can add his All-American name to the roll of legendary riders, an exclusively European list.

Only three cyclists have won four straight — France's Jacques Anquetil, Belgium's Eddy Merckx and Spain's Miguel Indurain. From 1991-95, Indurain won a record five consecutive titles. Merckx, Anquetil and France's Bernard Hinault also have won five, the record for overall victories.

If all goes as forecast, Armstrong could tie the Tour record next year amid the hype of the centennial celebration of the world's grandest bike race.

Rewards of success

Armstrong's fortune — and his celebrity entourage — have grown with his success.

He won his first Tour in 1999, capping his comeback from advanced testicular cancer.

Since then, Armstrong has become the all-time highest paid cyclist in the world. He earns $4 million annually from U.S. Postal, his cycling team. That's four times more than the next-biggest name in cycling, Germany's Jan Ullrich. Ullrich, the 1997 Tour champion, will miss this year's event because of a knee injury. He finished second to Armstrong in 2000 and 2001.

Armstrong also will earn $6 million in endorsements, from companies such as Bristol-Myers-Squibb, which manufactured the chemotherapy drugs that saved his life, to Coca-Cola, Nike and Trek, which makes the bikes Armstrong rides. Each of his deals includes a bonus for a Tour win, which could push his 2002 earnings up by a minimum of $1 million.

Armstrong's celebrity status has generated a number of celebrity friends.

People magazine recently noted that comedian and Academy Award-winning actor Robin Williams plans to visit Armstrong when the cyclist competes in the key Tour stages in the Pyrenees mountains later this month.

Williams is a huge cycling fan, and has flown to Austin the past two years to help support the Lance Armstrong Foundation's Ride for the Roses weekend, the organization's biggest annual fund-raiser.

President Bush has asked Armstrong to be on his newly created cancer panel.

"It might be the biggest honor I've ever received," Armstrong said.

Armstrong's popularity has grown to the point that he requires bodyguards during big events here and in Europe.

Warming slowly

The bodyguards, in particular, appear to have rubbed the French the wrong way.

Last year, Tour director Jean Marie Leblanc was publicly critical of Armstrong, describing his Tour bodyguards as "gorillas." Armstrong again will have a bodyguard for the Tour.

And because of his high profile, Armstrong has become less accessible to European cycling fans. This, too, makes some bristle.

"There was a story that Bernard Hinault had so many bruises on his back at the end of a stage because of all the spectators touching him," said Patrick Merle, a journalist with the French news service Alinea. "I don't think Lance has very many bruises."

"The French have never been keen on American culture, just on principle. The fact that Lance is a Texan, well, Texans are known to be more American than Americans. But I think the French have accepted Lance more this year. In every major interview he's given in France, he states that he loves the country. He's not the type of person to say 'I love you' just to get somebody to love him."

Armstrong hasn't expressed a lot of love for the French government or the French media. French authorities began investigating Armstrong's Postal Service team for drug use four months after he won the Tour in 2000. The investigation was prompted by a French television investigation. Reporters followed the Postal team doctor during the Tour and dug through trash, confiscat-

**ROBIN WILLIAMS AND LANCE ARMSTRONG SHARE A LAUGH
DURING THE 2002 RIDE FOR THE ROSES. THE PAIR BECAME
FRIENDS THROUGH THEIR LOVE OF CYCLING.**

"There is no reason to attempt such a feat of idiocy, other than the fact that some people, that is to say some people like me, have a need to search the depths of their stamina for self-definition. (I'm the guy who can take it.) It's a contest in purposeless suffering. But for reasons of my own, I think it may be the most gallant athletic endeavor in the world. To me, of course, it's about living."

LANCE ARMSTRONG ON THE TOUR DE FRANCE

LANCE ARMSTRONG IS ENJOYING HIS POPULARITY, ESPECIALLY WHEN IT HELPS RAISE MONEY FOR CANCER RESEARCH.

TAYLOR JOHNSON/AUSTIN AMERICAN-STATESMAN

ing empty boxes of Actovegin. The substance is not on the banned list, and its medical uses, if any, have been debated since the Postal investigation.

The French government announced last month that the investigation was nearing an end, and that there had been no evidence found to show that Armstrong or his teammates used performance-enhancers during the 2000 Tour.

"There's going to be a boring press conference (today) in Luxembourg — my God, what is everyone going to talk about?" Armstrong said of his pre-Tour press conference.

"The investigation is finished. We gave (the French government) everything they wanted, but they continue to drag their feet. They know they've lost. It's been a complete failure for them. . . . It's been a huge embarrassment for them, but I don't feel sorry for them."

Friends in high places
Armstrong said he will guard his time more closely this year after the Tour so he can spend more time with his growing family. Two-year-old Luke is "pedaling his butt off on his little BMX Trek," Armstrong said. Six-month-old twin girls, Isabelle and Grace, are starting to develop personalities. Along with his wife, Kristin, the Armstrongs split their time between Austin and Gerona, Spain, their European base.

Most of Armstrong's friends are the same ones he had before his October 1996 cancer diagnosis. But since he began winning his Tour championships, his social circle has expanded to include many famous people.

There's Williams, who left him a joke-laden voicemail in July 1999 to congratulate him on his first Tour victory. Armstrong listened to the message while riding in a limousine, then passed around the phone so his buddies could hear the message. Williams has made the Tour trip for the past two years.

Singer Lyle Lovett has grown close to Armstrong after he was the featured entertainer at Armstrong's party last

October to celebrate five years of being cancer free. And Armstrong has stayed at the Santa Barbara, Calif., home of actor Kevin Costner.

Armstrong made an unannounced visit to New York after the Sept. 11 terrorist attacks on the World Trade Center. He also visited several of the fire stations and rode bikes with rescue workers.

"I wanted to go because I love New York City," Armstrong said. "It's a great city, and in my opinion the grandest city in the world, full of tough people who were devastated. We went unannounced because I was not interested in a media event, but rather a personal goodwill mission."

When the New York mayor heard Armstrong was in the area, he invited him on a 20-minute helicopter ride with former President Clinton.

After Clinton met Armstrong, he asked him to dinner the next time the cyclist was in New York. That came in December, when Armstrong and his agent, Bill Stapleton, had paella with Clinton, daughter Chelsea and Academy Award winner Kevin Spacey.

"Lance still is always stunned at stuff like that," Stapleton said. "He always thinks, 'Why would someone like that want to have dinner with me?'"

Armstrong said he loves living in Austin because he can be normal here. The town has been supportive of Armstrong as well.

In April, the Ride for the Roses weekend raised $2.7 million. More than 9,000 fans showed up for a rock concert to kick off the weekend, and 6,600 cyclists were in the Ride for the Roses to end the festivities.

Armstrong's Foundation, which was created in 1997, has awarded more than $7 million in grants dealing with cancer survivorship issues.

"Austin is just a different type of city," Armstrong said. "The people are by far the most supportive bunch. I can lead a normal life and never have to feel funny. I can go out for normal things, like Mexican food, ice cream and a cold beer."

"I love this race from the very depths of my heart. It gives me motivation and it transcends me like nothing else in the world."

LANCE ARMSTRONG ON THE TOUR DE FRANCE

FIRST AND FOUR MOST
AUSTINITE IS FIRST AMERICAN TO WIN FOUR BACK-TO-BACK TITLES

SUZANNE HALLIBURTON
American-Statesman Staff

July 29, 2002

PARIS — Three years ago, as Lance Armstrong celebrated his first Tour de France victory with a ride on the Champs-Elysees, he was applauded more for his inspiring comeback frahe Texas flag for his stay, Armstrong read a congratulatory note from Gov. Rick Perry. The hotel previously had a rule allowing another country's flag to be flown only when a head of state was staying there. It amended the rule in 1999 for Armstrong's first victory and has flown the Lone Star flag for his annual visits.

Armstrong's victory earned him membership to an exclusive, previously all-European club.

Only three other cyclists, all of whom are considered legends, have won four Tours in a row: Frenchman Jacques Anquetil, Eddy Merckx of Belgium and Spain's Miguel Indurain. Indurain holds the record of five in a row, which he won from 1991-95.

Most cycling experts think Armstrong will roll into Paris a year from now with his fifth straight win, which would coincide with the Tour's centennial celebration.

"I think he can win five," Merckx said. "I see no real rival for him for the next two years."

As he has in the previous three, Armstrong dominated this Tour, with its 2,032-mile route that took the riders three weeks to complete. He won by 7 minutes, 17 seconds over runner-up Joseba Beloki of Spain.

The peloton, which started with 189 participants from 21 teams, dwindled to 153 by the end of the Tour.

The riders started in Luxembourg, spent a day passing through Germany, then came into France for the final 18 stages. The riders endured both the flat, windswept routes in Normandy and Brittany and the intimidating, mile-high mountain passes of the Pyrenees and Alps.

They also enjoyed the charm of riding past endless vineyards and fields of sunflowers and lavender before taking a high-speed train to Melun, a Paris suburb, on Sunday morning to begin the final stage.

Armstrong, who won four stages, unofficially clinched the Tour on July 21, on another unseasonably hot afternoon on top of Mont Ventoux, the giant, bald mountain of Provence. He had won two straight mountain stages, but his third-place finish so intimidated the field that Beloki, his main rival this year, waved the flag of surrender. He tried to keep up with Armstrong that afternoon but lost 1:45 to the champion over the last five miles of the stage.

"Armstrong is just too strong," Beloki said. "I'm going for second."

JOSEBA BELOKI OF SPAIN CONGRATULATES FOUR-TIME WINNER LANCE ARMSTRONG ON THE WINNER'S PODIUM AFTER THE 2002 TOUR.

"The record won't keep me here, happiness will."

LANCE ARMSTRONG

IT'S JUST LANCE ARMSTRONG, ALONE WITH THE
FANS, THROUGH THE PYRÉNÉES MOUNTAINS IN
STAGE 12 OF THE 2002 TOUR.

TAYLOR JOHNSON/AUSTIN AMERICAN-STATESMAN

The rest of the way, Armstrong and his U.S. Postal Service team, with riders from five countries on its nine-man roster, stayed conservative, knowing that the race was won. Team members laughed and cut up on the long, silver U.S. Postal bus, blasting the greatest hits of rock group ZZ Top before each stage.

Within the past week, Armstrong said, he started seeing many American and Texas flags along the Tour route. By Tour's end, there were thousands of Americans in Paris.

"This event definitely hasn't been Americanized," he said. "But, gradually, you've been seeing more Americans coming here for the race, especially in Paris."

"It's remarkable to see so many American flags, everywhere you look," added Johan Bruyneel, the Belgium-born team director of U.S. Postal. "That says a lot about Lance's popularity. The fans are very important to him. They're a big motivation."

Central Texas fans celebrated Armstrong's victory Sunday at the Hard Rock Cafe in downtown Austin. The celebration was sponsored by Capital Sports & Entertainment, the agency that manages Armstrong's business affairs.

However, Bill Stapleton, Armstrong's agent and founder of Capital Sports, said Armstrong will not immediately return to Austin for a celebration, as he has in previous years. Stapleton said Armstrong will fly to New York next Sunday for a race in Manhattan, then immediately return to Spain to spend August with his family.

Stapleton said Armstrong will return to Texas in September.

"He just wants to keep it low key," Stapleton said. "Next year, if he wins a fifth, it'll be a bigger deal."

Armstrong earned more than $300,000 for winning the Tour but will give the money to members of U.S. Postal. He already makes $10 million a year, including $6 million from endorsement deals.

But Armstrong is building more than a bank account. He's building a legacy.

Each year at this time, Armstrong has been asked to describe the mark he'll leave on the sport. His answer has been consistent.

"I know there's never been a Tour victory by a cancer survivor," he said. "Hopefully, that's what they'll remember me for."

"*Anything is possible. You can be told that you have a 90-percent chance or a 50-percent chance or a one-percent chance, but you have to believe, and you have to fight.*"

LANCE ARMSTRONG

RIDERS IN THE PELOTON CLIMB COL DU GALIBER. IN THE BACKGROUND IS ANOTHER MOUNTAIN IN THE ALPS, LA MEIJE. THE 16TH IS BY FAR THE TOUGHEST STAGE OF THE 2002 TOUR WITH THREE HUGE CLIMBS. IN ALL, THE RACERS HAVE TO CLIMB 15,351 FEET.

TAYLOR JOHNSON/AUSTIN AMERICAN-STATESMAN

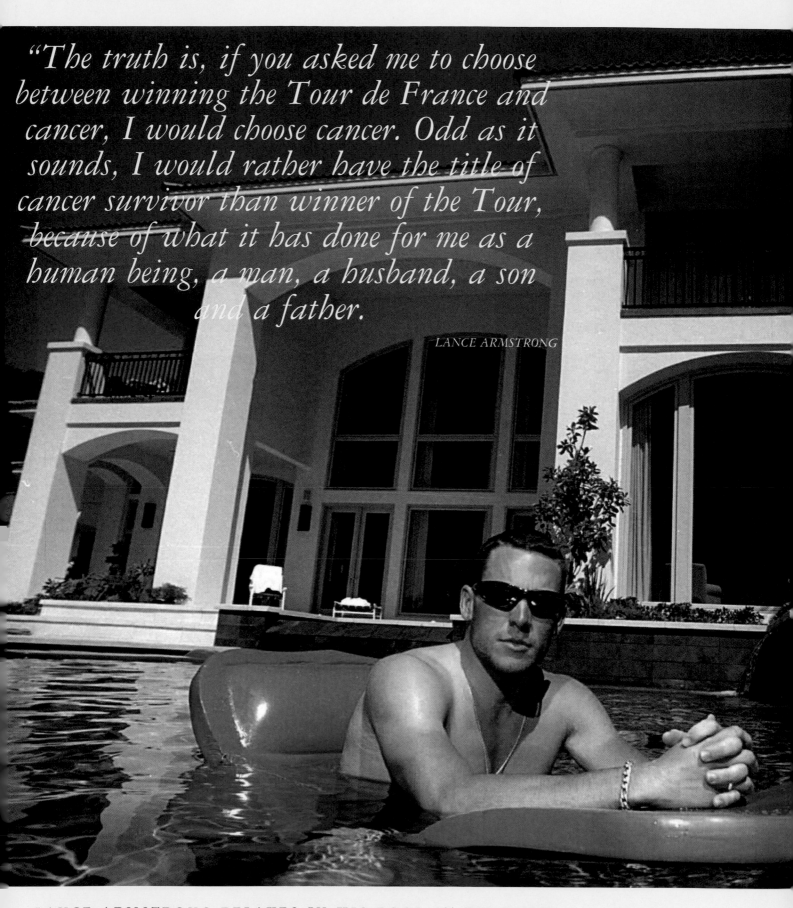

"The truth is, if you asked me to choose between winning the Tour de France and cancer, I would choose cancer. Odd as it sounds, I would rather have the title of cancer survivor than winner of the Tour, because of what it has done for me as a human being, a man, a husband, a son and a father.

— LANCE ARMSTRONG

LANCE ARMSTRONG RELAXES IN HIS POOL AT HIS HOME NEAR LAKE TRAVIS. ARMSTRONG HAS COME A LONG WAY SINCE HIS FIRST PROFESSIONAL RACE IN 1992.

LANCE ARMSTRONG'S LONG, WINDING ROAD

Tour de France champ is on top of the world, but it wasn't always so

SUZANNE HALLIBURTON
American-Statesman Staff

June 30, 2003

It's difficult to fathom — given that Austin's Lance Armstrong soon will be competing for legendary status in his sport of cycling — but go back to the beginning of his professional career, 11 summers ago, and realize that he had a tough premiere, hardly indicative of where he is now. The four-time defending Tour de France champion finished dead last in his first professional race, the Classico San Sebastian. Back in 1992, he was 20 years old, healthy and headstrong with a Texas-size chip on his shoulder. He also was a month removed from a 14th-place finish, impressive for an amateur, in the 1992 Summer Olympics in Barcelona, Spain.

The San Sebastian, a one-day classic race that took riders through Spain's picturesque Basque country, had seemed the perfect venue for Armstrong to prove to the European cycling community that he would be a longtime factor in their sport.

The race was a memorable event, mostly because the weather was atypical for August. It started hot and steamy, then turned cold and rainy. Eighty riders, made miserable by the conditions, abandoned the 120-mile race. A frustrated Armstrong crossed the finish line in 111th place, 27 minutes behind the winner.

WITH THE HELP OF LANCE ARMSTRONG AND OTHER CHARISMATIC RIDERS, THE TOUR DE FRANCE CONTINUES TO GAIN IN POPULARITY AND FANS LINE THE RACE ROUTE TO CHEER FOR THEIR FAVORITES.

RALPH BARRERA/AUSTIN AMERICAN-STATESMAN

He contemplated quitting cycling entirely and heading back to Texas. But he figured his mother would be angry, so he stuck with his plans — and eventually became the world's best rider.

Eleven years later, he laughs at the memory of his first pro race, pointing out that while so many riders "quit," he toughed it out.

Armstrong, 31, is by far today's best rider. He's still gutsy, healthy after battling advanced testicular cancer seven years ago, and headstrong.

And, as he prepares for his quest for a record-tying fifth consecutive Tour de France title, he also is an emerging legend.

"I don't know if I'll ever feel comfortable with the legend thing," Armstrong said. "Hopefully, it's my personality not to think that way. Probably, because I'm from Texas and not Europe, I don't have a full appreciation of cycling (history). But I'm not resting on the fact that I've won a few Tours."

This year's Tour, which starts Saturday at the base of the Eiffel Tower in Paris, will be steeped in history. After all, it's the centennial celebration of the world's grandest bike race, which began as part of a circulation war between two French newspapers, L'Auto and Le Petit Journal.

Back in 1903, Henri Desgrande, who worked for L'Auto, created an endurance race that would take riders in a clockwise, 1,500-mile route through France, hitting the major cities of Paris, Lyon, Marseille, Bordeaux and Nantes.

The inaugural Tour doubled the circulation of L'Auto. And today, it's the most attended sporting event in the world, with an estimated 15 million people watching the race unfold over 2,130 miles and 21 days.

Every day, fans from all countries line the route that will take the 198 riders, as it did a century ago, from Paris clockwise around France. The cyclists will take on the flat lands of Champagne country, then head east for the Alps along the French-Swiss border. They'll turn south, eventually hitting the imposing Pyrenees near Spain before heading north to flatter land along the

Atlantic coast. Then it's back to Paris on July 27 for a largely ceremonial ride into the City of Lights and onto the finish line on the Champs Elysees.

All those major stops from a century ago will be included on the route, along with the quaint towns nestled among the lavender and sunflower fields and the lush vineyards that give France its vibrant color in the middle of summer.

If Armstrong is successful in the Tour — and he's again heavily favored — the victory will place him in the rarified company of Eddy "The Belgian Cannibal" Merckx; famed Frenchmen Jacques Anquetil and Bernard Hinault, and Spain's Miguel Indurain.

Those four cyclists co-own the Tour record with five career wins each. The reclusive Indurain, still a huge hero in his country, won his in succession from 1991 to 1995, giving him the record for most consecutive Tour victories. Armstrong can tie him this year.

Chris Carmichael, Armstrong's longtime coach, knew that his star cyclist had the talent to win a single Tour way back when Armstrong's results weren't as spectacular as they are now. Stringing together several Tour wins was never given much thought until 2000, when Armstrong successfully defended his 1999 victory, which seemed so improbable at the time.

"I never said, 'Guy, you're going to be a legend.' But I knew his capabilities," Carmichael said. "If I told him he was going to be the next Miguel Indurain, then I would have been almost dooming him for failure."

In late January, Armstrong's attention was diverted from his Tour training when he and his wife, Kristin, separated. She stayed at the couple's home near Lake Austin. He moved to a cabin west of Austin that the family had used as a getaway.

Lance left for the couple's home in Girona, Spain, in late February, days after the couple publicly announced their separation. Kristin and the couple's three children — 3-year-old Luke and 18-month-old twins Grace and Isabelle — remained in Austin.

A month after Lance left, Kristin moved the children to Spain and back into the couple's home. The couple has

A YOUNG FAN SHOWS HER SUPPORT OF LANCE ARMSTRONG.

DEBORAH CANNON/AUSTIN AMERICAN-STATESMAN

"I think it's important to be understood, to be honest, to be hard working, and ultimately the press, the public, the organizers . . . they'll decide. But I can only be myself. I can't be the guy that goes out and puts on a show . . . I can only be myself."

LANCE ARMSTRONG

been working to reconcile their marriage since then.

Kristin Armstrong declined to comment about the reconciliation.

"As for personal questions about our marriage, it's best to leave that alone, I think," Kristin Armstrong wrote in an e-mail to the *American-Statesman*.

"Everything is fine," Lance Armstrong said last week.

Professionally, Armstrong's life has never been better. His annual earnings, which include his salary from the U.S. Postal Service Pro Cycling Team and endorsements, will bring him $15 million this year. His salary of $4 million makes him the highest paid cyclist in the world. He's believed to make more than four times what Germany's Jan Ullrich earns. Ullrich, the 1997 Tour champion who finished runner-up to Armstrong in 2000 and 2001, is expected to be Armstrong's greatest challenge this year.

In addition, Armstrong's exposure in the United States is at an all-time high.

"Over the past year, Lance has reached a new level in the marketing world," said Bill Stapleton, Armstrong's Austin-based agent, "as evidenced by the major television advertising campaigns we saw in Comcast, Coca Cola, and his newest partner, Subaru."

Earlier this year, Armstrong signed a five-year, $12 million contract with Subaru to be their national spokesman. He is the main focus of the carmaker's "Driven by What's Inside" marketing campaign. Armstrong's six commercials will appear on all networks and 36 cable channels.

Armstrong already is a spokesman for Bristol-Myers Squibb — which manufactured the chemotherapy drugs that helped save his life in 1996 — as well as Coca-Cola and Nike. He also appeared in commercials in 22 western markets for Comcast, which purchased AT&T Broadband last year.

And, in October, Armstrong's new book, *Every Second Counts*, will go on sale. His first book, *It's Not About the Bike*, has been a national bestseller in hardcover and paperback.

The public exposure only will increase if Armstrong wins his fifth Tour.

"I feel so good. I feel so strong," Armstrong said. "I still haven't won five in a row. I've always been careful not to claim victory too quickly. I have won four. And that is what it is."

> *"I wasn't desperate
> for a stage win.
> I wanted to get to
> the finish line in one
> piece and preserve
> the victory."*
>
> — LANCE ARMSTRONG

LANCE READY TO TAKE 5

*Rival's fall all but assures
Armstrong of Tour de France victory*

SUZANNE HALLIBURTON
American-Statesman Staff

July 27, 2003

NANTES, France — With several yards to go before the finish line Saturday afternoon, four-time defending Tour de France champion Lance Armstrong finally allowed himself to acknowledge his place in sporting history. It had been three long, energy-sapping weeks. And during that time, Armstrong had persevered through two crashes, avoided another mishap that knocked out a significant challenger and overcome a bout of dehydration so severe he almost had to abandon the race with eight stages to go before its conclusion in Paris.

DARK CLOUDS DURING THE PROLOGUE INDIVIDUAL TIME TRIAL FORESHADOWED THE GRUELING RACE AHEAD OF LANCE ARMSTRONG IN 2003.

LANCE ARMSTRONG HOLDS UP FIVE FINGER—ONE FOR
EACH TOUR DE FRANCE VICTORY—BEFORE BEING AWARDED
THE YELLOW JERSEY DURING STAGE 19 OF THE 2003 TOUR.

RODOLFO GONZALEZ/AUSTIN AMERICAN-STATESMAN

But while coasting into Nantes late Saturday afternoon, the Austin resident smiled broadly, briefly ignoring the rain for the first time all afternoon. He then let loose of his right handlebar, clenched his fist and shook it at no one in particular.

Later, as he stepped to the podium as the Tour's overall leader, he waved five fingers — celebrating what is almost certain to be his fifth straight championship — and threw his bouquet of yellow roses and mums into the crowd as if he were a young bride tossing a bouquet.

He had finished third in the time trial, but the placing didn't matter. The 11 seconds he gained on Jan Ullrich, his main competition for the yellow jersey, were the sweet prize.

"I wasn't desperate for a stage win. I wanted to get to the finish line in one piece and preserve the victory," Armstrong said after increasing his overall lead to a comfortable 1 minute and 16 seconds.

Barring a catastrophic crash in the final stage, Armstrong will step to the podium again at about 10:30 this morning Texas time. What he clinched in the rain Saturday afternoon will finally become official as the 2,130-mile race ends with a ceremonial ride past the Arc d'Triomphe on the Champs-Elysees.

More than 100,000 fans will celebrate the Tour's centennial and Armstrong's historic feat as the riders take 10 laps on Paris' most famous boulevard. To this point, only Spain's Miguel Indurain has won five Tours in a row, doing so during 1991-95.

In this bike race, which started as a publicity stunt a century ago, only three other riders — France's Jacques Anquetil and Bernard Hinault and Belgium's Eddy Merckx — have won five championships, but they didn't do it consecutively. All but Anquetil, who died 16 years ago of cancer, are expected to be on hand for today's parade honoring the Tour's past champions.

For Armstrong, this Tour proved to be his toughest. It also proved to be the sixth-closest since World War II, considered the Tour's modern era.

"To be this close, I think it feels better than all the others," Armstrong said.

Previously, Armstrong's smallest margin of victory came in 2000, when he beat Ullrich by 6:02. The last time a Tour came down to the final weekend was in 1989, when American Greg LeMond came from behind to beat France's Laurent Fignon in the final stage — a short time trial in Paris. LeMond won his first Tour championship by eight seconds in the closest Tour in history.

Armstrong's battle with Ullrich wasn't quite as tight as the LeMond-Fignon duel. Before Saturday's individual time trial, 1 minute and 5 seconds separated the two riders.

In a time trial, unlike other stages, riders race by themselves against the clock. They receive no help from their teammates. Each of the 148 riders still remaining of the 198 who started the Tour three weeks ago in Paris began the time trial two minutes apart.

The start was in Pornic, a small town on the coast of the Atlantic Ocean. The finish was in Nantes, an industrial port city on the mouth of the Loire River. Despite the rainy conditions that lasted throughout the day, thousands of fans lined the road, cheering wildly.

In the four previous Tours he has won, Armstrong took all but two of the time trials. However, Ullrich beat him by 1:36 eight days ago. With a similar performance Saturday, Ullrich, the 1997 Tour champion and two-time runner-up to Armstrong, could have seized the yellow jersey.

If dry, the course, with its wide roads and gradual turns, is considered an easy one built for speed. However, the rain and gusty Atlantic winds turned it treacherous.

Ullrich, who was forced to ride aggressively in an attempt to catch Armstrong, fell victim to the road.

With six miles to go before the finish, Ullrich leaned into a turn but took it too fast. His back wheel skidded out from underneath him, and he slid on his right side into a barrier.

The crash badly scratched his right leg, but with the help of a team official following in a car, Ullrich got back on his bike and tried to make up the time he had lost, estimated at 11 seconds.

But Armstrong's advantage was too great, and both riders eased up near the finish line. Armstrong finished 14 seconds behind stage winner David Millar of Scotland and nine seconds behind American Tyler Hamilton.

Ullrich was fourth, 25 seconds out of first place. Today, he will most likely finish second in the Tour for the fifth time.

"I feel a little sad," Ullrich said. "It would have been a dream to put on the yellow jersey."

LANCE ARMSTRONG LEADS THE PELOTON AS THEY MAKE
A TURN NEAR THE TOWN LA BASTIDE DE BOUSIGNAC, FRANCE,
IN 2003'S STAGE 13. ARMSTRONG KEPT THE YELLOW JERSEY
JUST AHEAD OF TEAM BIANCHI'S JAN ULLRICH.

"At some point, there will be a time for me to say, no more Tours de France, but that will be at the same time I say no more cycling."

LANCE ARMSTRONG

**LANCE ARMSTRONG HONORS TEAM
BIANCHI'S JAN ULLRICH (LEFT)
AND TEAM TELEKOM'S ALEXANDRE
VINOKOUROV (RIGHT) DURING THE 2003
PODIUM CEREMONY IN PARIS.**

RODOLFO GONZALEZ/AUSTIN AMERICAN-STATESMAN

A TUMBLE TURNED INTO TRIUMPH

Courageous win in mountains was pivotal in drive for fifth title

SUZANNE HALLIBURTON
American-Statesman Staff

July 28, 2003

PARIS — The highlights and hardships were many for Lance Armstrong as he won a fifth straight Tour de France championship. He overcame crashes and near-crashes, stomach flu, dehydration and hard-charging rivals.

In fact, this Tour held so many surprises for Armstrong that before he set off for Paris in Sunday's final stage, he said, "If a plane landed in the race, I wouldn't be surprised."

But the stage that set him rolling toward his latest championship, which he celebrated Sunday on the Champs-Elysees, came a week ago and involved the Tour's most difficult stage.

That day, the cyclists competing in Stage 15 had to climb two massive peaks in the Pyrenees — the infamous Col du Tourmalet and then the summit of Luz Ardiden, two climbs rated as "beyond classification" by Tour organizers. Before Armstrong and his handful of challengers encountered those two passes on the 99-mile route, they also had to get over the Col d'Aspin, a very difficult, category one climb.

Entering the stage, Armstrong had only a 15-second lead over Germany's Jan Ullrich and an 18-second edge on Alexandre Vinokourov of Kazakhstan. He had lost 1:36 to Ullrich two days before in an individual time trial, then dropped another 19 seconds to the German rider the next day in the Tour's first stage in the Pyrenees.

And Armstrong still was reeling from the severe dehydration he suffered in the 100-degree-plus heat of the time trial. He felt it most in his legs, and for the first two mountain stages in the Pyrenees, he stayed on Ullrich's wheel, allowing Ullrich to dictate the pace of the leader's group.

Armstrong was suffering, but trying to persevere. Johan Bruyneel, the team director for Armstrong's U.S. Postal squad, said: "Lance never knows when he's been beaten."

He knew that when he stayed even with Ullrich at the finish of last Sunday's stage that he could clinch the Tour title Monday afternoon.

Unlike previous days, the temperatures dropped into the 50s for the critical Stage 15. Fog settled in at the summit of Luz Ardiden. On the Col du Tourmalet, Ullrich tried to force the issue by attacking early. Armstrong was forced to answer. Absent his Postal teammates, he was isolated against Ullrich and Spanish riders Iban Mayo and Haimar Zubeldia.

So on the closing six-mile climb to the summit, Armstrong largely went alone, without a strong leadoff from teammates Jose Luis Rubiera and Manuel Beltran. Armstrong followed the attack of Mayo, which also was answered by Ullrich.

A young boy, holding a yellow cloth bag thrown out as a souvenir by the Tour's publicity caravan, stepped out on the road to cheer the riders. The bag's handle caught Armstrong's right handlebar, and he crashed hard on his left side. Ullrich waited for Armstrong to right himself. Armstrong, after riding for another 300 yards, missed a pedal and fell hard into the frame of his bike.

He righted himself again and zoomed away. Ullrich couldn't follow. At one point of the stage, Armstrong owned a lead of 1 minute. He crossed the finish line 40 seconds ahead of Ullrich, and with the time bonus for winning the stage, added 52 seconds to his overall lead.

"At the end, that's where I knew it was enough to win the Tour," Armstrong said Saturday.

"Giving up was never an option."

— *LANCE ARMSTRONG*

ARMSTRONG NOW FINDS HIMSELF IN ELITE COMPANY

Having met toughest test yet, Lance will try for elusive sixth title

JOHN MAHER
American-Statesman Staff

July 28, 2003

After crashing, bonking, dehydrating and scrambling like crazy, Lance Armstrong somehow found the will to win one of the wildest, most-inspiring races in the 100-year history of the Tour de France. Armstrong now has two things in common with cycling immortals Jacques Anquetil, Eddy Merckx, Bernard Hinault and Miguel Indurain: All share the record of five Tour victories. And none has won a sixth.

At least, not yet.

Armstrong will attempt to do so next year, hoping his strengths will overcome the weight of history and his own advancing age.

All of the other five-time winners, legends who left their contemporaries slack-jawed with awe, tried for that elusive sixth win. For three, that Tour proved only to be their swan song. Merckx alone made two futile runs at history before realizing the sixth victory was forever beyond his grasp.

For most of the great riders, the fifth Tour win came as hard as it did for Armstrong. Anquetil won his first Tour in 1957 by a cozy margin of 14 minutes and 56 seconds. In 1964, he finished only 55 seconds ahead of arch-rival Raymond Poulidor in winning his final Tour title.

In 1974, Merckx took his fifth Tour only after catching Poulidor on one death-defying descent that is still the stuff of Tour legend. In 1985, Hinault joined the elite group because his main threat, Greg LeMond, was a teammate who was ordered to stay in his place.

This year, Armstrong, used to winning by six and seven minutes, had to wait until the final time trial to secure a victory over a revitalized Jan Ullrich.

Late in the three-week race, Armstrong observed, "It has been a Tour of many problems, close calls and near-misses. It seems it has been a lifetime, and I wish it would just stop."

It could have been one of Armstrong's easiest wins with the way the field managed to deplete itself. The third-place and fifth-place finishers from 2002, Lithuanian Raimondas Rumsas and Spaniard Igor Gonzalez de Galdeano, weren't on hand. The second-place finisher in 2002, Joseba Beloki, eventually went out in a nasty crash. The fourth-place finisher from 2002, Santiago Botero, was among those who badly overestimated their own form, a group that included such supposed threats as 2003 Tour of Italy champion Gilberto Simoni, 2003 Tour of Italy runnerup Stefano Garzelli and reigning Tour of Spain champion Aitor Gonzalez. In addition, the top two American threats, Tyler Hamilton and Levi Leipheimer, the eighth-place finisher in 2002, suffered serious injuries in a horrific crash in the first stage of the 2003 race.

Hamilton bravely rode on, but the realistic challengers to Armstrong were soon down to a Ullrich and the aggressive Alexandre Vinokourov, from Kazakhstan. Only when he finally found his old form did Armstrong put them away.

"What makes a great endurance athlete is the ability to absorb potential embarrassment, and to suffer without complaint. I was discovering that if it was a matter of gritting my teeth, not caring how it looked, and outlasting everybody else, I won. It didn't seem to matter what sport it was — in a straight-ahead, long-distant race, I could beat anybody. If it was a suffer-fest, I was good at it."

LANCE ARMSTRONG

LANCE ARMSTRONG POSES FOR A PICTURE WITH FELLOW FIVE-TIME WINNERS (FROM LEFT) BERNARD HINAULT, EDDY MERCKX AND MIGUEL INDURAIN.

Assessing Armstrong's performance, Gonzalez de Galdeano observed in a Web diary, "In previous Tours he was so superior that the bad days were not noticed."

Next year there should be more serious rivals for Armstrong. With him finally showing signs of vulnerability, it's likely more teams will attempt to build real threats to him and his U.S. Postal teammates, instead of settling for the occasional meaty scrap of a stage win.

History, after all, suggests that Armstrong's days are numbered. None of the other five-time winners was able to win beyond the age of 31. Armstrong will be 32 next year, almost 33. In the past 50 years, only one winner, Dutchman Joop Zoetemelk, who was 34 in 1980, won the Tour beyond the age of 32.

Armstrong's age may be deceptive, however. Past Tour de France champions would routinely race in at least one of the other big European tours each year. Anquetil made the podium at the Tour of Italy six times, winning twice, and he won the Tour of Spain in 1963. Indurain won the Tour of Italy twice, while Hinault won three times in Italy and twice in Spain. Merckx was a five-time winner of the Tour of Italy and won that race in 1973, when he also won the Tour of Spain — and then skipped the Tour de France.

Armstrong, who met Arnold Schwarzenegger after one stage this year, is cycling's Terminator. The Tour de France is what he does. It's all he does. The rest of his short competitive season is training and preparation for the one big cycling race that matters to the American public and his sponsors. That's one big edge he has on his peers who all cracked while going for a sixth Tour triumph.

Once Anquetil fell behind in the 1966 race, he didn't follow Poulidor's reckless descent down a mountain. "I'm not going to kill myself in my last year on the Tour," he reasoned.

In 1986 Hinault was grudgingly forced to admit that LeMond was the better rider, and Hinault retired soon thereafter. And in 1996, Indurain cracked during the brutal opening time trial.

Merckx was punished by the mountains in his final two Tours. After his first failed attempt to win his sixth Tour title, he said, "Miracles don't exist in sports. It's always the strongest who wins."

Once more that was Armstrong. The peloton believes it is closing the gap, but only next year's race will tell.

IN HIS YELLOW JERSEY, LANCE ARMSTRONG MAKES A TURN ALONG THE CHAMPS-ELYSÉES DURING ONE OF 10 LAPS MADE ALONG THE FINAL STAGE OF THE TOUR DE FRANCE TO COMMEMORATE THE 100-YEAR ANNIVERSARY OF THE EVENT.

RODOLFO GONZALEZ/AUSTIN AMERICAN-STATESMAN

"I read his first book, got a bike and lost 50 pounds."

ANITA HARTGRAVES, FIFTH-GRADE TEACHER

HE INSPIRES PEOPLE
Cyclist's fans hit pavement hours before book signing

RALPH K.M. HAURWITZ
American-Statesman Staff

October 10, 2003

Veronica Laduc admires Lance Armstrong. So much so that she got in line at 5 a.m. Thursday at Book People downtown for the international cycling champion's 8 p.m. book signing. She was happy to wait 54,000 seconds to get his autograph on a book titled *Every Second Counts*.

"I know it's ridiculous," said Laduc, 33, a computer systems analyst who was equipped with a folding chair, sandwiches, a water bottle, a rain poncho and a cheerful attitude. "I didn't want to take any chances. He inspires people with his sense of courage."

She was the first in line, but other Armstrong fans soon joined her, many of them reading the book, Armstrong's second, to while away the time. The early birds, all women, also compared notes on which bicycles they own.

"I read his first book, got a bike and lost 50 pounds," said Anita Hartgraves, 48, a fifth-grade teacher who drove from Corpus Christi for the event. "My mother has ovarian cancer, and he's an inspiration to us that she's going to get through this."

Melissa Siebrecht, 23, who teaches music theory, came to see "a legend in the making."

Austin resident Armstrong, a cancer survivor and American icon, has vowed to pursue a sixth Tour de France victory next year. That would give him more wins than anyone else.

"He's kind of a great role model for Americans abroad. He's just a gentleman," Siebrecht said.

Stephanie Jett, 26, got in line 12 hours before Armstrong was due to arrive because she regards him as someone who knows what's important.

"I'm a respiratory therapist and deal with life and death every day," Jett said. "He can appreciate life."

Alex Pippard, the bookstore's events coordinator, said autograph seekers were allowed to form a line early because "we didn't want a line for the line. It's kind of neat, the sort of temporary community they form out there."

YOUNG FANS SEEK AUTOGRAPHS FROM LANCE ARMSTRONG.

DEBORAH CANNON/AUSTIN AMERICAN-STATESMAN

TEAM U.S. POSTAL SERVICE CELEBRATES ATOP THE PODIUM AFTER WINNING THEIR FIRST TEAM TIME TRIAL DURING STAGE 4 OF THE 2003 TOUR DE FRANCE HELD AT SAINT DIZIER. THE TEAM CONSISTS OF (FROM LEFT) VICTOR HUGO PEÑA (BEHIND GIRL) JOSE LUIS RUBIERA, ROBERTO HERAS, FLOYD LANDIS, LANCE ARMSTRONG, PAVEL PADRŇOS, VIATCESLAV EKIMOV, GEORGE HINCAPIE (BEHIND EKIMOV) AND MANUAL BELTRAN.

"I had learned what it means to ride the Tour de France. It's not about the bike..."

LANCE ARMSTRONG

ARMSTRONG CYCLING THROUGH PUBLIC LIFE

Promotional travel, divorce may be Tour champ's toughest ride

SUZANNE HALLIBURTON
American-Statesman Staff

October 24, 2003

Here's a small slice of Lance Armstrong's life, months after the Austin rider became only the second cyclist ever to win a fifth consecutive Tour de France. You take a private jet to New York on Monday evening so you can catch a flight to Paris on Tuesday morning. You stay there for two days, having dinner with your team's European sponsors and appearing at a press conference Thursday morning announcing the route for what could be your record-breaking sixth straight Tour victory. Then you take an 11-hour plane trip back to Austin that night, hoping the jet lag isn't bad enough to keep you from fully participating in this weekend's Ride for the Roses, the main annual fund-raiser for your Lance Armstrong Foundation.

Last week there were TV interviews with David Letterman and Charlie Rose and an appearance on *Today*. You also throw in a appearance on Don Imus' radio show.

The week before it was an appearance on Jay Leno's show and a kickoff party in Los Angeles for the Tour of Hope, the 3,230-mile, coast-to-coast charity ride to focus more attention on cancer research and survivorship issues.

Earlier this month, you made an inspirational speech ($150,000 per appearance) to company workers in Calgary, Alberta. You'll do the same next month for a company in Dallas. Then it's a meeting of the president's cancer panel in Birmingham, Ala.

Then there were the book signing sessions in Austin, New York and Washington, D.C., and an upcoming one in Los Angeles for your second autobiography, which premiered at No. 4 on *The New York Times* bestseller list.

And, when you're home, you're the proud father, coaching your 4-year-old son's soccer team while watching your twin, soon-to-be 2-year-old girls develop their own distinctive personalities. Spending time with the three kids, after all, is the main reason you've altered your training plans for next year's Tour.

"I've been kind of busy," Armstrong deadpanned this week. "I've been doing a lot of traveling."

This year has been one of physical travel and emotional upheaval for Austin's best-known citizen this side of Michael Dell. Armstrong, who turned 32 last month, won his fifth straight Tour in July by 61 seconds, one of the smallest margins in history, a physically demanding victory that wasn't assured until the Tour's final weekend.

Armstrong almost quit the three-week-long race during the first time trial in southern France, when he suffered such dehydration in the 100-plus heat that he had blurred vision miles before the finish line.

Hours after he stood on the podium in Paris, he was thinking about how he could change his preparations for 2004.

"In hindsight, I probably didn't work as hard as I

LANCE ARMSTRONG SPENDS A FEW MINUTES WITH HIS SON LUKE BEFORE THE START OF THE FIRST STAGE OF THE 2002 TOUR DE FRANCE.

should have," he said. "I'll go back to work and be more focused. I didn't do the stretching, the exercises, that kind of stuff as well as I could have. I just slipped a bit. But it was a good slip, because now I know how focused I need to be."

Two weeks after he returned from his European base in Spain in late August, he and wife Kristin decided to end their five-year marriage. Lance moved into a house in the same Central Austin neighborhood as Kristin so he could be closer to his children.

He declined this week to comment on his divorce.

This month, his primary focus has been promoting his book, *Every Second Counts*, the follow-up to *It's Not About the Bike*, which chronicled his recovery from cancer and his rise to Tour de France champion. It sold 1 million copies worldwide.

"Based on the numbers I've been seeing, the new book is doing twice as well as the first one," said Bill Stapleton, Armstrong's friend and agent.

In December, Armstrong's U.S. Postal team will meet in Austin for a weeklong training camp. For now, he's trying to ride where he can, and he jogs about 45 minutes a day when he's on the road. He took part almost every day in the Tour of Hope, when each of the 26 participants rode 120 miles.

Armstrong is enjoying himself, eating well and drinking the occasional beer. He can gain up to 15 pounds in the off-season but will whittle his weight to the low 160s by next summer.

He recently got out his bike and took a spin through New York's Central Park.

A bike courier rode alongside him and challenged Armstrong to a race. Armstrong won. "But he was close," the Tour champion said, pausing for a long laugh. "He just wanted me to give a little bit, so he could show me what he had."

Armstrong will move to Spain in February to train for two months, then return to Austin for April and May so that he can spend time with his children, who for the first time in their lives will not spend the spring and summer in Europe.

He's also contemplating whether the 2004 Tour will be his final one.

"I don't know, I really, really don't know," he said. "I'd say there's about a 50-50 chance this will be my last one."

**TAKING A FEW MINUTES
OUT OF HIS BUSY DAY,
LANCE ARMSTRONG ANSWERS
QUESTIONS FROM THE MEDIA.**

TAYLOR JOHNSON/AUSTIN AMERICAN-STATESMAN

"The Tour is too special to me. It means more than any other race."

LANCE ARMSTRONG

KELLY MYERS, FROM CORSICANA, TEXAS, WAITS PATIENTLY FOR LANCE ARMSTRONG TO RIDE PAST.

LANCE ARMSTRONG RELAXES BY THE POOL, TAKING TIME OFF FROM A BUSY TRAINING SCHEDULE.

KAREN WARREN/AUSTIN AMERICAN-STATESMAN

KIDS KEEP THE TOUR TRAINING AT HOME

Since divorce, Armstrong spending more time in Austin

SUZANNE HALLIBURTON
American-Statesman Staff

April 18, 2004

Four-year-old Luke Armstrong wants to help each morning as his father prepares for work. That's why when Lance Armstrong hops on the saddle of his bicycle, readying for a day of intense training, his oldest child helps push him out the door. Armstrong's 2-year-old twin girls also are starting to understand what Daddy does for a living. "They recognize my bike clothes as my work clothes," Armstrong said this week as he drove to his ranch in Dripping Springs.

This time of year, the five-time defending Tour de France champion typically is in Europe, training near Barcelona or racing in Belgium and the Netherlands. But this spring is unique, as Armstrong tries to train for the Tour and handle the responsibilities of being a single father.

His three children are living in Austin with their mother, Kristin Armstrong, following the couple's divorce in December.

To be near the children, Armstrong scrambled the focus and logistics of his training schedule as he prepares for what would be an historic sixth straight Tour victory this July.

For the sake of the children, he's racing less and training more.

"I miss my kids," he said. "Either way (with or without the children), I know I'd be focused. But I miss my kids."

After competing in the Criterium International in France in late March, Armstrong flew back to Austin to spend at least a month on his home turf. He's ridden in

"I miss my kids. Either way (with or without the children), I know I'd be focused. But I miss my kids."

LANCE ARMSTRONG

Central Texas and in California, where his team annually conducts a preseason training camp.

Saturday night, Armstrong attended his annual "Live to Ride Gala," a fund-raiser and awards ceremony for his foundation, at the Austin Convention Center. Today he leaves for Atlanta. On Tuesday, he and seven teammates from his U.S. Postal team will compete in the six-day Tour of Georgia, Armstrong's first domestic stage race since he started his French winning streak.

Sometime in late April or early May — Armstrong hasn't decided exactly when — he'll fly back to his European home in Girona, Spain. He only has one more competition, the Criterium du Dauphine Libere, in France from June 5-12 before the Tour kicks off in Liege, Belgium, on July 3. The month of May and most of June will be dedicated to training for the Tour time trials and stages in the Alps and Pyrenees.

Chris Carmichael, Armstrong's long-time private coach, said the cyclist's training is ahead of schedule from this time a year ago, and so far he hasn't suffered from a lack of actual competition.

"There are advantages to both — just training and racing," Carmichael said. "The advantages of getting the racing in now is that you get a feel for the race pace, race tempo, race intensity. But the advantage of just training is you get to isolate a key area."

In recent days, Armstrong has concentrated on his climbing skills, including 10 hours a week of high-intensity pedaling when his heart rate is 160 beats a minute. By July, his heart rate will escalate to 185 when he is riding all out in a climb or time trial.

Johan Bruyneel, Postal's director, is with the rest of the team in Spain. He and Armstrong speak at least once a day, if not more. Bruyneel will join Armstrong in Georgia.

"The training is not that much different," Bruyneel said. "A few years ago, Lance would always go back to the U.S. in April for the Ride for the Roses, rush back and ride Amstel Gold Race (in the Netherlands) and Liege-Bastogne-Liege (in Belgium). I think that was not optimal.

"He had a first good block of training and racing in Europe, and now a good training cycle in the U.S. We've never experienced this schedule before, but I have a good feeling about it, and I like it."

Armstrong's top Tour competition — Germany's Jan Ullrich, Spain's Joseba Beloki and Tyler Hamilton of the United States — are gradually rounding into shape, but they will be racing in more events leading up to the Tour than Armstrong.

"My form is coming along," Hamilton wrote last week in his Internet diary. "But as we say here in Espana, poco a poco. Little by little."

Ullrich, the 1997 Tour champion who has finished as runner-up to Armstrong three times, including last year, recently has been criticized by a cycling heavyweight for being too lax in his training.

Belgian Eddy Merckx, a five-time winner of the Tour and perhaps the best cyclist ever, told the German news service Deutsche Presse Agentur, "It seems that Jan has again not worked hard enough in his previous preparation and is still too much overweight. Sure, he still has over two months, but to beat Lance Armstrong in the Tour will be harder than 2003."

The shuffling of his training probably is a better fit for Armstrong. After all, he's always insisted that he preferred training to competing in races other than the Tour.

"Training, you can control your own destiny," he said. "When you're racing, your destiny is in the hands of 200 other guys, so you're at the mercy of 200 other guys. I'm probably not ready to go all out."

**LANCE ARMSTRONG AND THE
U.S. POSTAL SERVICE TEAM RIDE ON A
COUNTRY ROAD EAST OF AUSTIN, TEXAS.**

"This is not a final exam you can cram for. This is the Tour, and it requires a yearlong commitment. You come here in the month of May when it's a ghost town, and you simply ride up and down the mountain."

— LANCE ARMSTRONG

**THE PELOTON, OR PACK
OF RIDERS, STRETCHES AS
FAR AS THE EYE CAN SEE.**

DEBORAH CANNON/AUSTIN AMERICAN-STATESMAN

TOUR FOR DUMMIES

AMERICAN-STATESMAN STAFF

July 2, 2004

The Tour de France is such a foreign event to American fans, who seem to appreciate Lance Armstrong's achievements yet don't know what to make of a sport that doesn't require a ball, a bat, a net or an end zone. So as Austin's Armstrong gears up for a possible record-setting sixth Tour championship, here are some tips, explanations of various rules and some insight into what's going on in the peloton — er, the main pack of riders.

Call it our very own Tour for Dummies.

So what is a peloton, and how do I buy one?

"Peloton" is a French word from which the English "platoon" is derived. It describes the main mass of riders.

The field, except for a few look-at-me guys, stays together for much of a flat stage. You will not see significant breaks in the peloton until the Tour reaches the mountain stages; there, the strong mountain riders (like Lance) will pull far away from the flatland lovers.

After a hundred miles of riding, it seems that most of the riders end up with the exact same time in a lot of stages. Why?

As long as there's not a significant gap — defined as more than a second — in the peloton as the group finishes a stage, everyone receives the same time as the winner, although he may finish second or 181st.

Why does Lance always finish so far back the first week?

Armstrong and his main challengers, cyclists such as Jan Ullrich, Tyler Hamilton and Iban Mayo, don't sweat the early stages. Those flat stages are the domain of the sprinters, whose sole aim is to finish first for a brief moment of glory and a nice payday.

But Armstrong and the challengers will ride toward the front of the peloton during these stages. No one wants to be caught up in a crash, which can cause cyclists to fall like a row of dominoes. Odds suggest that staying near the front of the group protects you.

Armstrong is interested in his overall time, and there's little to be gained on these stages when the entire peloton can finish within seconds of the winner.

The only stages where a rider can put time on the rest of the field are the time trials and ones in the mountains.

Why do they put time on trial?

The time trial is called the "race of truth." Those two stages literally pit an individual rider against the clock. Each rider starts at a different time and receives no help from his teammates.

Except . . .

Except in the team time trial. On that day, entire nine-man teams ride together against the clock, working like a finely tuned orchestra as each team member takes a turn at the front of the pack to knife through the wind. Everyone on the team is awarded the time of the fifth-place teammate.

Why can't someone other than the team leader compete for the yellow jersey? I mean, is this a team or individual sport?

Both.

Each team has nine members. Before the Tour starts, each team declares a leader. For U.S. Postal, that's obviously Armstrong. In most cases, the other eight riders are there to help the team leader. They are called domestiques.

Domestiques, who often command six-figure salaries, serve as worker bees who do most anything during the

Tour. They set the pace at the head of the peloton. They ferry food and water to their team leader.

Sometimes, they provide a wheel for the leader if he has a flat. And in rare cases, they'll surrender their bikes if the leader has a mechanical problem.

Teammates also allow the leader to draft off of them and save energy for a final attack.

Why are there time limits for stages?

It seems incomprehensible that a one-minute margin can decide the winner of a 2,100-mile, three-week race, but the competition is that close.

One big reason: To keep competing every stage, a rider can't have a daily time more than 10 percent slower than the winner. Judges can waive this rule on certain occasions, such as in 2001 when Armstrong, Ullrich and the rest of the peloton finished more than 35 minutes behind a group of 11 who had broken away on a rainy, cold day. Armstrong made up that margin in the mountains, and none of the 11 finished among the top three overall.

Do they stop at McDonald's along the way?

No, but cyclists do eat during the stages, which take four to six hours to complete. The feed zone usually begins about 30 miles into the stage and stops about 12 miles from the finish. The feed zone changes somewhat in the mountains.

Each cyclist receives a musette bag, filled with energy bars and glucose drinks.

What about bathroom breaks?

When you've gotta go ...

Two choices for those who must go: Stop and lose time, or just go as they ride. These are pros. Don't try this on Loop 360.

Why is their lots of preening and kissing on the podium every day?

The yellow jersey isn't the only shirt up for grabs every day.

Sprinters want to secure the green jersey.

The top climbers want to wear red-and-white polka dots, signifying that they are King of the Mountains.

The best young riders under 25 want to sport the white jersey.

Sometimes teams have more than one goal coming into the Tour. Take Germany's Team Telekom. They'll ride so that Ullrich can yank the yellow away from Armstrong. But they'll also ride in hopes of Erik Zabel gaining the green.

Oftentimes, the green jersey isn't decided until the final sprint on the final stage in Paris. That's been the case the past two years. The sprinting jersey is decided on a points system, with points gained by winning intermediate sprints (won by the first person reaching certain intervals) or an overall stage. It's the same for the mountain winner. The wearer of the white jersey will be the highest-ranking youngster in the standings.

The standings for each jersey are updated daily, starting with the prologue, the short time trial that kicks off the Tour. It's solely contested so that Stage 1 will have riders wearing coveted jerseys. There is a podium presentation every day for each jersey, complete with bouquets of flowers and kisses from models.

What are the so-called rules of the peloton?

Riders follow strict, unwritten rules of conduct. Usually, it's up to the most dominant cyclist to make sure the rules are followed.

If the yellow-jersey wearer has pulled over to go to the bathroom, no one in the peloton is allowed to make his move, or attack.

If the yellow jersey crashes or has a flat, no challenger is allowed to take advantage, unless it's obvious the yellow jersey is out of the race. This is why there was such a discussion last year about whether the challengers to Armstrong slowed enough when he crashed in the Pyrenees. Armstrong got on his bike and won the stage. Hamilton, an old teammate with U.S. Postal, rode to the front of the leaders' group and forced Ullrich and Mayo to slow down.

What are attacks?

It sounds like something out of a war game, but cycling is all about attacking.

You'll see that some cyclists will attack, or breakaway early, in a stage. Mainly, these guys are trying to help their sponsors get their logos on television, because

ARNOLD
SCHWARZENEGGER
PRESENTS LANCE
ARMSTRONG WITH
THE YELLOW
JERSEY DURING THE
STAGE 11 CEREMONY
OF THE 2003 TOUR.

RODOLFO GONZALEZ/AUSTIN AMERICAN-STATESMAN

rarely do these early breakers win the stage.

Toward the end of a flat stage, say about 18 miles out, the team that is trying to set up their rider for victory will increase the pace of the peloton.

The final few kilometers of a flat stage are beautiful in their precision. Each team's rider will take a pull at the front, riding as fast as he can before dropping back in exhaustion.

The next rider does the same thing, until it's time for the chosen one, who has been drafting this whole time, to take the race. He'll jump out as if popped from a slingshot.

Oftentimes, a 100-mile stage will be decided by the length of a wheel.

It's a different story in the mountains.

Typically, the key attack comes on the final mountain pass, which is so steep that it's difficult for even a small car to climb it, much less a worn-out cyclist. The best cyclists wait to attack when all the challengers are suffering the most and not capable of following or keeping up with the action.

What's the winner get for all that work?

He'll get a check — 400,000 Euros (or about $500,000) to the yellow jersey winner. But that's chump change. Armstrong's money — he made an estimated $16 million is 2003 — comes from bonuses from his team and individual sponsors that kick in with a Tour championship.

NO ONE HAS WON SIX TOURS

Here's why

SUZANNE HALLIBURTON
American-Statesman Staff

July 2, 2004

For the past several weeks, Lance Armstrong has been as antsy as a teenage boy before his first junior race. Every day, someone — a reporter, a fan, an opposing cyclist, the baker down the street — would ask Armstrong about No. 6.

As in a sixth Tour de France title. As in the record for most victories in the world's toughest sporting event.

He'd have his pat answer handy. "Not thinking about it," he'd say in English or French or Spanish.

But he has been thinking about it, or at least trying to avoid the thought. "I'm getting superstitious so I don't want to talk about it," he said last week.

Armstrong, who announced in June he plans to compete in 2005 for (dare anyone say?) a seventh championship, is uncomfortable musing about his legacy when he has yet to retire.

Four of the most famous cyclists in history — France's Jacques Anquetil and Bernard Hinault, Belgium's Eddy Merckx and Spain's Miguel Indurain — all won the Tour de France five times. All tried for No. 6 and failed. Indurain, like Armstrong, won his five titles in a row.

Given that history, the number six has become almost mythical, unapproachable, as if its been coated in gold and diamonds, sealed in thick glass and put in a museum.

"The Tour de France is always difficult, even if you only win it once," said Merckx, who twice tried for a sixth title. "I don't believe in a six-time jinx. . . . That nobody won a sixth is coincidence, but if Lance doesn't make it, then maybe there is something in the air.

"Of course riding all these Tours takes a toll on your body and your mind."

LANCE ARMSTRONG HAS CREATED A PLACE FOR HIMSELF IN
CYCLING HISTORY WITH HIS CONSECUTIVE TOUR VICTORIES.

Age-old questions

There is no underlying superstitious reason for the lack of a sixth title, just a simple physiological one — age.

It takes equal parts talent and experience to win and survive the rigors of a race that lasts for three weeks and traverses more than 2,000 miles, with routes in the tallest mountains and flattest plains, in searing heat, December-like chill, rain, wind and fog. Usually, a rider wins the event when he's in his mid- to late 20s when his mental toughness finally catches up to his talent. Armstrong won his first Tour at 27.

"The Tour de France, in my opinion, is the most grueling sporting event in the world. There's really nothing else like it," said American Tyler Hamilton, a challenger to Armstrong who, at 33, will be one of the oldest in the field of 189 riders.

"That's why there have been so few riders who've dominated the race with five wins. Six wins would be . . . an incredible human achievement."

As they grow older, champions can keep their focus. Yet these same titans lose their ability to bounce back from seven-hour days on the bike. Armstrong estimates he's off his bike only 10 days a year. In-season training rides are seven hours; easy days, meant to keep the muscles loose, are two hours.

Armstrong said it takes him a month, if not two, to recover from riding in the Tour.

Riding strong, riding smart

At some point, the talent tops out — Armstrong conceded he hit his zenith in 2001 — and the goal becomes to ride smart, then hang on as the younger guns attack and press for the podium.

None of the four previous five-time winners claimed yellow after the age of 31. Dutchman Joop Zoetemelk, who at 34 won the Tour in 1980, was the oldest champion in the past half-century. Armstrong is two months shy of his 33rd birthday.

"When you get older, sometimes your body doesn't respond to training the way you anticipate," said Chris Carmichael, Armstrong's longtime private coach who rode in the 1986 Tour. "The amount of load, the training you put on an athlete starts to dip. . . . I don't think you necessarily get stronger doing those things."

Armstrong, acknowledging his age, simply wants to be as good as he has been, which has been more than enough to keep winning.

"I feel strong; I feel good," Armstrong said. "I'm not improving. But I think I am as strong as I have been in the past."

History tells us a lack of motivation becomes a factor in No. 6. Bad luck plays a part. And sometimes, the graying champions can't keep out of the way of the upstarts.

1960s: Anquetil calls his shot

Anquetil, the jaunty Frenchman who swilled champagne as often as he drank water, couldn't accomplish six titles. After winning in 1957, 1961, 1962, 1963 and 1964, Anquetil skipped the 1965 race and tried one more time in 1966.

No cyclist before him had won more than three titles since the event started in 1903 as a publicity stunt by a French newspaper. If he couldn't win six, Anquetil wanted to make sure that his hated rival Raymond Poulidor, a fellow Frenchman, wouldn't don yellow.

"If by some chance I don't win the Tour, he won't win it either," Anquetil proclaimed before the race, not caring whom he offended.

Anquetil, who won his first Tour at 22, stayed complacent while riding for No. 6. Poulidor — who with seven career podium finishes is known in cycling as always the groomsman, never the groom — tried valiantly for the jersey. He finally cracked in a final Alpine stage. The next day, Anquetil withdrew, knowing that France's Lucien Aimar had secured the title.

1970s: Kicking the Cannibal

Then came Merckx, known as "The Cannibal" for his ability to chew up competition. The Belgian won his first title in 1969 by nearly 18 minutes, claiming all three jerseys, the leader's yellow, green for top sprinter and polka dot for best climber. He won a stage by 8 minutes on an 87-mile solo break.

He also won the next three years and again in 1974, skipping 1973 because "the French didn't want me to come," recalled Merckx.

In 1975, Merckx appeared set for No. 6. In much the same way the media is doing now with Armstrong, reporters pondered whether Merckx had the motivation and ability. Still, he wore yellow halfway through the Tour.

THE PELOTON RIDES THROUGH THE FIELDS OF THE THUIN REGION DURING THE 2ND STAGE OF THE 2004 TOUR DE FRANCE.

But with less than a half mile to the finish line to Puy de Dome, Merckx was struggling to maintain his lead over eventual champion Bernard Thevenet of France. Then came one of the most blatant unsportsmanlike events in Tour history. As Merckx passed, a Frenchman rushed out of the throngs lining a mountain path.

"A fan kicked me in the belly on a mountain stage," said Merckx, who finished second in 1975. "I lost too much time and my liver suffered throughout the whole Tour. I understand Lance when he tries to be nice to the French. When they don't like you, they really don't like you.

"Afterwards I came back for one more — in 1977 — but I was beaten and ended up sixth."

1980s: LeMond plays spoiler

In 1986, Hinault tried for No. 6, after wins in 1978, 1979, 1981, 1982 and 1985. But he was forced to give in to teammate Greg LeMond, the first American to win the Tour. After LeMond took the lead in the mountains, Hinault gave one final run for yellow, chasing the American up L'Alpe d'Huez. But Hinault could only keep up, not put time on his young rival.

Near the finish, Hinault grasped LeMond's hand to congratulate him, and LeMond pushed Hinault forward so that he could have the victory on one of the most mythical of Tour stages. Hinault won the polka-dot jersey as King of the Mountains.

1990s: Last assault on 6

Indurain and Jan Ullrich, the German who is expected to be Armstrong's biggest obstacle to six, are similar in their long bodies and riding styles. When Indurain won his five in a row from 1991-95, he beat his competition not by sudden bursts up a mountain, but by maintaining such a fast pace that his challengers were forced to drop back. Ullrich also has that style.

In 1996, when he was gunning for six, oddsmakers proclaimed Indurain an overwhelming favorite. But he couldn't keep up on the first mountain stage and effectively blew his chance for No. 6.

Denmark's Bjarne Riis, who is now the team director for CSC, won that Tour, with Ullrich picking up his first of five runner-up finishes. Indurain was 11th.

Armstrong concedes he's not much into the history of his sport, although he does know the big names. He recently went to Merckx, his longtime friend and consultant, for advice on how to deal with the stomach-gnawing pressure that comes with trying to rewrite history.

Knowledge of it doesn't keep the pressure at bay.

"I just want to get this race started," Armstrong said.

THE PRESS FIRES QUESTIONS AT
LANCE ARMSTRONG BEFORE THE
FIRST STAGE OF THE TOUR.

"He's an example to everyone who never believed they could do it . . . whatever IT is . . . you CAN do IT!"

FAN QUOTE

CAN LANCE ROLL TO RECORD SIXTH STRAIGHT TOUR DE FRANCE VICTORY?

AMERICAN-STATESMAN STAFF

July 3, 2004

Lance Armstrong should take a tip from baseball great Leroy "Satchel" Paige when he begins his hunt for a sixth consecutive victory in the Tour de France, the World Series and Super Bowl of bicycle racing. "Don't look back," Paige said. "Something may be gaining on you." In Armstrong's case, "something" is more than the other riders in the Tour: It's vulnerability (he barely won last year's race), age (he'll be 33 in September) and controversy (a new book alleges that he used banned performance-enhancing drugs).

Some cycling experts already are counting Armstrong out before the 21-day event that begins today. And Armstrong, who has been having a heightened celebrity existence this year with rock star girlfriend Sheryl Crow, hasn't been impressive in the Tour warm-up races.

Armstrong's many critics are saying he's too old, past his peak, out of shape and not ready for the grind that is the Tour de France. Plus, the rules have changed for this 91st anniversary race. Among them, the stage races that Armstrong excels in have been moved to the end of the Tour.

Beyond all that, Armstrong's most dedicated challenger, German rider Jan Ullrich, is riding well this year and is almost certain to push the challenge for the yellow victory jersey.

But don't count Armstrong out just yet. He has a powerful will, and a man who beat cancer to win five consecutive Tours shouldn't be too airily dismissed. And the drug-use allegations he vehemently denies — he's one of the sporting world's most drug-tested athletes, and he's never failed — could be the spur he needs to ride for a record sixth-straight win.

He can be dangerous because so many people are doubting him this year. Those doubts can be a powerful incentive — not that making history by being the only rider to win six consecutive Tours isn't. None of the world's great cyclists — Miguel Indurain, Greg LeMond, Eddie Merckx — has been able to win the Tour six consecutive times.

There is drama to burn in this year's race, almost all of it centered on Armstrong. That's a lot of baggage to carry up the Pyrenees and Alps and across France to the victory platform in Paris.

But Armstrong has already proved he is capable of amazing feats. One more won't come as that great a surprise to those who have followed his amazing career.

"*Cannot lose. Too strong.*"

FRENCH CABBIE ON LANCE ARMSTRONG

MUCH LOVE FOR LANCE, IN TEXAS AND FRANCE

KIRK BOHLS
American-Statesman Staff

July 14, 2004

GUERET, France — I joined the Tour de France on Tuesday and brought favorable news to Austin's favorite son from the nation's capital. France has surrendered.

Already, if unofficially.

For the sixth year in a row, Lance Armstrong has won this country's most celebrated sports event. At least, he has in the hearts and minds of Parisians who worshiped the very ground that five-time Tour winners Jacques Anquetil and Bernard Hinault rode on.

In four rain-swept days in Paris, my wife, Vicki, and I asked everyone we saw for their impressions of the American cyclist in his quest for history.

Waiters. Clerks. Hotel attendants. Cabbies. Regular Joes and Josephines. Even a tourist from Israel who was more interested in Bush vs. Kerry than Armstrong vs. Ullrich.

"Good guy, Lance Armstrong," the rotund waiter with the mischievous eyes at Jardin Notre Dame restaurant said on a rainy Sunday evening. "He's nine miles back, but he's still going to win his sixth Tour."

"He will win," the postal clerk said at the Louvre.

"Cannot lose," according to the cabbie from de Gaulle Airport. "Too strong."

"Do you have a horse?" the souvenir stand attendant at Cluny-Sorbonne said.

OK, so everyone isn't as clued in to this race. Meaumeau had a steed of his own and was aghast that a Texan wouldn't own one.

Everywhere else it was the same response. Armstrong, once reviled in this country for his Texas-sized arrogance

**LANCE ARMSTRONG AUTOGRAPHS
A T-SHIRT FOR A LUCKY FAN.**

DAVE CWIKLINSKE, OF SWINDON, ENGLAND, AND KARIN GOULD,
OF PITTSBURGH, PENNSYLVANIA, SHOW THEIR SUPPORT FOR LANCE
ARMSTORNG AND THE U.S. POSTAL SERVICE TEAM.

and the suggestion of drug use that has been totally unfounded, has been elevated to exalted hero.

Armstrong would hear none of it, and that's exactly what is driving this 32-year-old physical specimen with the unquenchable desire. Don't tell him the race is over.

"Oh, no," a confident yet superstitious Armstrong protested as we met outside his shiny U.S. Postal Service bus. "That's not right. Too far to go."

So he'll be more careful than cunning in his assault on the history book, even if the French are all but resigned to watching Armstrong ride first down the Champs-Elysees in two weeks.

The French haven't had one of their own ride down that street as the champion since 1985, when Hinault won for the fifth and final time.

They seem generally awestruck by Armstrong's talent and will. Perhaps they are still a bit reluctant to fully embrace him as they would a famed countryman, but they seem willing at long last to recognize him as a true champion.

Some things are undeniable. Like the fact you have to beg for butter with your bread, and water fountains exist only in front of monuments. And you must get accustomed to the showers with the small glass partition at Hotel Galileo that allows for a standing water in the bathroom.

Galileo was to astronomy as Armstrong is to cycling, but it would have been nice if the Italian scientist had discovered at least one ice machine among all those constellations.

Along the streets are almost no signs that the Tour will be ending in Paris on July 25. In fact, the lone sports billboard of any kind on the walls of the city's clean and reliable underground Metro system hinted at the Olympic track trials later this month.

But Paris loves a parade and promises to throw a humdinger in two weeks. They will practice today in honor of Bastille Day, commemorating the start of the French Revolution, when a mob attacked the antiquated Bastille prison and found just seven prisoners to free from the 100-foot towers.

This country could have a long wait before one of its own cyclists stages a similar revolution and frees the race from Armstrong's hold.

LANCE ARMSTRONG—THE PRIDE AND JOY OF AUSTIN, TEXAS,
AND THE U.S.—IS ONE OF AMERICA'S TOP ATHLETES.

TAYLOR JOHNSON/AUSTIN AMERICAN-STATESMAN

*"He is gentlemanly and heroic;
a very likeable combination."*

FAN QUOTE

WHERE ARMSTRONG RANKS AMONG SPORT'S GREATS — NEAR THE TOP

KIRK BOHLS
American-Statesman Staff

July 2, 2004

If Lance Armstrong rides down the Champs-Elysees later this month, decked out in the yellow jersey for the sixth consecutive year, he will only cement a legacy that is already imbedded into the sports consciousness of a nation obsessed with its athletic heroes. His place in history has long since been made secure. But to what extent would his glory extend? To what would six straight victories in the grueling Tour de France possibly compare?

It's really impossible to say, given the degree of difficulty of the three-week race through the countryside and up and down the mountains of France, but it's safe to assume Armstrong will take a place alongside other icons in their respective sports.

Armstrong has had the national and international appeal and the endurance of a Richard Petty, long known to his legion of fans as The King of NASCAR racing. Like Armstrong, Petty proved himself over time with more than 200 career victories on racetracks across America, including seven checkered flags at the Daytona 500.

Like Petty under his trademark cowboy hat, Armstrong's lean look and focused stare excites millions, and his prowess has endeared him to cycling fans worldwide.

Armstrong has been at the top of his game and set the bar in cycling as the premier wide receiver Jerry Rice has in his. Not forecast to be a future Tour winner when he emerged out of Plano, Armstrong's career can draw some strong parallels with that of Rice, who wasn't even the first wide receiver picked in the 1985 draft out of obscure Mississippi Valley State. Rice was taken after Eddie Brown's and Al Toon's names were called.

Likewise, six-time Cy Young Award winner Roger Clemens has unique talents and has been recognized as the hardest-training player in baseball. The former University of Texas right-hander didn't stop once he reached 300 wins, pacing the Houston Astros in victories and showing no signs of slowing down at age 41.

Clemens, Rice and Armstrong are obsessive trainers in the off-season and bring to their sports the ultimate in competitive training. Rice wasn't the fastest receiver (4.6 seconds in the 40-yard dash), but he has scored more touchdowns than anyone in NFL history with 204. And after 19 pro seasons, he hasn't stopped yet.

Cycling isn't recognized as a contact sport, but when Armstrong survived everything from diarrhea to road rashes to dehydration during last summer's 61-second victory, he proved he can overcome any physical maladies and remain in championship form.

Armstrong doesn't have near the same build as Eric Heiden, the muscular speedskater from Wisconsin whose powerful 27-inch thighs were almost as thick as his waist. Heiden was best known for his five individual gold medals in the 1980 Winter Games at Lake Placid, but he'd won speedskating world titles starting in 1977 at age 18.

Like Armstrong, Heiden was an intense competitor and trained up to five hours a day when he took up the sport seriously when he was just 14. Coincidentally, Heiden eventually turned to cycling and competed in the 1986 Tour de France before a dangerous crash ended his race.

Six straight Tour wins would separate Armstrong from four other five-time winners — Jacques Anquetil, Eddy Merckx, Bernaud Hinault and most recently Miguel Indurain. Like them, Armstrong has stood the test of time and demonstrated the stamina and staying power to remain at the highest level.

Armstrong is in the same league as Byron Nelson, the gentleman golfer from Dallas who played in 133 tournaments in the 1940s and, in a staggering feat, won 11 consecutive events, including the PGA Championship, in 1945. Considered the father of the modern golf swing, Nelson had an eye-popping scoring average of just under 67 strokes during that run.

For sheer longevity, Armstrong's streak of six would compare favorably to the unprecedented Iron Man streak of Cal Ripken Jr., the Baltimore Orioles shortstop who didn't sit down for 2,632 straight games.

Ripken not only surpassed Lou Gehrig's record of 2,130 games but played five more seasons in a row without fail until he took himself out of a game against the visiting Yankees on Sept. 20, 1998. Armstrong's hardiness provides an equal example as a testament to blue-collar work ethic.

Even Joe DiMaggio's 56-game hitting streak in 1941, considered virtually unbreakable to this day, could be used as a measuring stick to gauge Armstrong's impact.

Armstrong would find good company in two-time Olympic gold medalist Edwin Moses, who rewrote the record book in the 400-meter hurdles when he set an amazing record and won 122 straight races in his specialty over nearly 10 years. That kind of dominance set him apart as one of track's all-time greats.

Houston's Carl Lewis deserves similar credit for his nine gold medals stretched over four Olympic Games, including four golds at the 1984 Games in Los Angeles to equal the 1936 feat of Jesse Owens. When he took home his ninth and final gold in the long jump at Atlanta in 1996 at age 35, he etched his name alongside track immortals.

It's not that crowded a pedestal Armstrong figures to share.

It's the highest platform on which any athlete could hope to stand and one that this lithe Texan with the incomparable drive plans to climb by being the fastest to Paris on July 25.

**LANCE ARMSTRONG RESTS IN HIS
HOME NEAR LAKE TRAVIS.**

ARMSTRONG CONTINUES MOUNTAIN WINNING STREAK

*He looks unbeatable in his quest for a record six
Tour de France championship.*

BY SUZANNE HALLIBURTON
American-Statesman Staff

July 21, 2004

L'ALPE D'HUEZ, France — Lance Armstrong's epic stage victory Wednesday, which all but guaranteed he will be the grandest champion in Tour de France history, actually started three months ago, when the Alpine passes thawed and cleared of slush.

Back when only one or two fans were watching — not the estimated 1 million who were here Wednesday — the five-time Tour champion and his U.S. Postal Service teammates rode the 9.6-mile route up L'Alpe d'Huez for three days. Eight times they climbed the 3,700 feet to the summit and traversed the 21 switchbacks on one of the most imposing mountains ever on a Tour de France route, knowing that Wednesday's mountain time trial could be the critical stage in Armstrong's quest for a record sixth Tour title.

That preparation paid off in a big way Wednesday, as Armstrong crossed the finish line with the second-fastest time ever for a climb of L'Alpe d'Huez.

He was so dominating that Jan Ullrich, who finished in second place, lost 61 seconds to his rival. And Italy's Ivan Basso, who started the time trial two minutes ahead of Armstrong, found himself passed along the way, now almost four minutes behind Armstrong in the overall standings.

"I think our secret is we work all year long," Armstrong said. "I hate to disappoint the skeptics. The secret is hard work. This isn't like a final exam that you can cram for. It's the Tour de France. It requires a year-long commitment."

In winning Wednesday to claim his third straight mountain victory, Armstrong looked as strong as he did in 2001. That's the Tour he recently described as the strongest of his five-year championship reign. He also beat Ullrich by 1 minute in a similar Alpine time trial in 2001, the last time the Tour included such a stage in its three-week itinerary. And he also won the stage to Alpe d'Huez.

"I don't know if he is as strong as he was in 2001," Postal team director Johan Bruyneel said. "But today, Lance was impressive."

By stage end, Armstrong owned a 3 minute, 48 second lead over Basso, the lead rider for Team CSC of Denmark. Germany's Andreas Klöden, a teammate of Ullrich's on T-Mobile, was third, 5:03 out of first.

Ullrich, who has finally ridden well these past two mountain stages after a disastrous first two weeks, moved from fifth to fourth, 7:55 out of first.

The 1997 Tour champion and five-time runner-up has never finished lower than second in Paris, but that streak obviously is in danger. Ullrich realistically can make up ground only in two of the remaining four stages — Thursday's final mountain route and Saturday's individual time trial on flat ground.

The 159 riders who have survived the first 2 1/2 weeks of the Tour started Wednesday's time trial in reverse order based on their overall standing. That meant Armstrong had the advantage of starting last at Bourg d'Oisans, with Bruyneel giving him updates by radio as

LANCE ARMSTRONG CELEBRATES HIS RETURN TO THE YELLOW JERSEY AFTER FINISHING STAGE 15 FROM VALREAS TO VILLARD-DE-LANS OF THE 2004 TOUR DE FRANCE.

his challengers reached the intermediate time checks.

Ullrich had the fastest time at every checkpoint until Armstrong eclipsed them.

"Lance was super strong today," said CSC team director Bjarne Riis. "But that wasn't a surprise. Beating Ullrich by a minute was a surprise."

Basso, who was eighth Wednesday, remains the only rider who could knock off Armstrong, but even that is only a remote possibility after Wednesday.

The 26-year-old Italian rolled out of the starting gate two minutes ahead of Armstrong. With roughly a mile to go before the finish, Armstrong made up that 2-minute gap and passed his friend.

"I wasn't happy with my performance, but I wasn't too sad. For some reason I didn't feel too good. I lost a lot of time to Armstrong, but not to the others below me. Lance proved to be the strongest rider in the peloton."

Basso will try to attack Thursday in the final Alpine stage — a 127-mile route from Bourg d'Oisans to Le Grand Bornand with three "Category 1" climbs and an even tougher "beyond classification" ascent of the Col de la Madeleine roughly 30 miles into the stage.

The cyclists raced on a road so congested it was difficult for them to pass, even with a team-car escort. Fans from numerous countries lined the crooked road, with many American and Texas flags on display.

The spray-painted messages on the road — usually positive messages to cheer on a rider — turned negative, many of them directed toward Armstrong. He said he heard the most negative words from German fans, some who had T-shirts printed saying that Ullrich would beat Armstrong by five minutes.

"They motivated me more than anything," Armstrong said with a devilish grin.

His teammates took the jeers another way, as a strong indication their leader will wear yellow in Paris on Sunday.

"They want to see a new champion," said Jose Luis Rubiera, one of Armstrong's mountain lieutenants. "But they know Lance is the best and he has been for six years."

LANCE ARMSTRONG SPEEDS TOWARD THE FINISH OF THE 2004 TOUR'S 16TH STAGE INDIVIDUAL TIME TRIAL FROM BOURG D'OISANS TO L'ALPE D'HUEZ, RETAINING THE YELLOW JERSEY.

DEBORAH CANNON/AUSTIN AMERICAN-STATESMAN

THE U.S. POSTAL SERVICE TEAM
SURROUNDS LANCE ARMSTRONG
AS THEY COAST THROUGH THE
18TH STAGE OF THE 2004 TOUR.

ARMSTRONG DENIES REPORT THAT THIS IS LAST TOUR

'I can't imagine not coming back here next year,' defending champion tells Statesman

SUZANNE HALLIBURTON
American-Statesman Staff

July 23, 2004

LONS-LE-SAUNIER, France — Amid speculation that he won't return to the race next year, Lance Armstrong told the American-Statesman today that he can't imagine this being his last Tour de France.

He categorically denied a report that he had already informed Tour officials of his intention not to return next year.

"Honestly, that's really not true," Armstrong said in a phone interview after today's Stage 18 of the Tour de France.

The three-week event ends Sunday in Paris, and Armstrong holds a commanding lead en route to his record sixth consecutive Tour title.

"I can't imagine not coming back here next year," Armstrong said. "This is the event that motivates me the most. It's my favorite race and the biggest race."

Armstrong has signed on with a new sponsor, the Discovery Channel, for 2005 after the U.S. Postal Service declined to renew its cycling sponsorship.

Armstrong, however, did not commit to riding in the Tour de France again, saying that he and his team will not make out their 2005 racing schedule until December.

"I'm just trying to get through this one," Armstrong said.

Armstrong promised that, out of respect for the event, he would work with Tour officials as he makes his decision for 2005.

Race director Jean-Marie Leblanc said he had heard only media reports regarding Armstrong's future at the race and not heard directly from the cylist or his team.

A CHAMPION CHARITY

Like its founder, foundation for cancer survival thrives

ANDREA BALL

American-Statesman Staff

July 24, 2004

Seven years ago, the Lance Armstrong Foundation was a fledgling charity with big dreams and a little money.

The nonprofit organization — founded in 1997 by Austin cycling sensation and cancer survivor Lance Armstrong — had one employee. It awarded one grant. And it had one mission: to fight urological cancers.

Today, the Lance Armstrong Foundation is an internationally recognized organization with 45 employees that is expected to raise $21 million by the end of the year. Last year, it paid out $3.6 million in grants to 80 cancer-related organizations around the country. It also has a $2.9 million endowment to ensure future income.

It took some growing pains to get this far. The foundation struggled with its mission, faced a changing office culture, and went through several leadership changes.

But those new-kid-on-the-block days are over. At least one charity watchdog group says the Lance Armstrong Foundation is as good as it gets.

"They are doing phenomenally," said Trent Stamp, executive director of Charity Navigator, a New Jersey-based group that evaluates nonprofit organizations. "The Lance Armstrong Foundation is about as tough to beat as Lance Armstrong himself."

Armstrong's high profile career, fueled by his remarkable battle against cancer, has led to a very high-profile life. The cyclist, on the verge of his sixth Tour de France championship, now stars in Nike commercials, appears on talk shows and graces national magazine covers.

That celebrity has been a boon to his foundation. The group expects to earn $7 million this year just through the sale of yellow wristbands engraved with Armstrong's mantra: Live Strong.

And those wristbands are everywhere. Some of Armstrong's Tour competitors, including Italian Ivan Basso, have been sporting them. This week, actor Matt Damon wore one on the "Late Show with David Letterman." And talk show host Jay Leno has been distributing the wristbands to his studio audience since the beginning of July.

If Armstrong clinches a record-setting sixth Tour victory on Sunday, as expected, the foundation will probably reap the benefits, Stamp said.

"They're raising a ton of money," he said. "One can only imagine that if he wins this next (Tour), the money will keep pouring in in record numbers."

From the beginning

Armstrong was 25 years old when he was diagnosed with testicular cancer in October 1996.

The cancer, the most common found in men ages 15 to 35, is usually treatable and has a 90 percent cure rate. But by the time the cyclist was diagnosed, the cancer had spread to his abdomen, lungs and brain.

Obviously, he survived.

In 1997, Armstrong volunteers started a foundation to raise money for testicular cancer research. The board of directors was a group of 15 professional and civic leaders. Many were friends and cyclists.

"One of the things that struck me, other than our cancer connection, was how authentic Lance was and how

**LANCE ARMSTRONG AND HIS FOUNDATION
HAVE RAISED MILLIONS OF DOLLARS TO
FUND CANCER RESEARCH.**

sincere he was about wanting something good to come out of it," said former Austin Mayor Kirk Watson, a former board member and a cancer survivor.

Those early days came with uncertainty. The group didn't have specific goals, detailed plans or much experience, said Jeff Garvey, an Austin entrepreneur who has been on the board since 1997.

"When the foundation started in the fall of 1997, we had $10,000 in the bank, no experienced employees and an idea," he said. "It would be going overboard to say we had a mission."

That first year, the nonprofit group held its Ride for the Roses bicycle rally and sponsored a medical symposium. The group raised about $240,000 and had one part-time employee.

Its first office was an 1,100-square-foot yellow house in downtown Austin.

For years, the foundation survived with a few paid employees and dozens of unpaid volunteers. Between 1997 and 2001, the organization went through two executive directors: John Korioth and Karl Haussmann, both cyclists and friends of Armstrong's.

"When he was starting this, Lance turned to the people he knew, his friends," Haussmann said. "We just sort of raised our hands and said, 'We'll help.'"

By 2001, the foundation was moving away from its initial mission. Instead of solely tackling urological cancer research, the group began to focus on surviving cancer, said Doug Ulman, the foundation's director of survivorship.

Modern medicine had created millions of cancer survivors, he said. But there were few resources to help people with the aftershocks of the disease, such as infertility, scarring, depression and family and employment issues.

Today, there are 10 million cancer survivors in the United States.

"We realized we had a larger opportunity than with just urological cancers," Ulman said.

In January 2003, Eileen Oldag — who for eight years had served as the executive director of Caritas of Austin — took over as the group's executive director.

Donations continued to climb. In 2003, the foundation received $8.8 million in contributions. The group paid out $3.6 million to 80 organizations focused on quality-of-life issues for people living with and through cancer.

LANCE ARMSTRONG—HERE DURING THE 2004 TOUR'S 18TH
STAGE—HAS USED HIS SUCCESS AND POPULARITY WITH FANS TO
FIGHT CANCER BY RAISING MONEY TO FUND RESEARCH GRANTS.

A SMALL SEA OF YELLOW HATS SITS ATOP CHILDREN WAITING
FOR THE FINISH OF STAGE 18 OF THE 2004 RACE.

DEBORAH CANNON/AUSTIN AMERICAN-STATESMAN

Recipients included the American Red Cross, Children's Hospital of Los Angeles and Indiana University.

In September 2003, Oldag left the organization for personal reasons. In January, the group replaced her with Mitch Stoller, former executive director of the Christopher Reeve Paralysis Foundation.

Smart growth

The foundation plans to use its money to grow programs and build its endowment, Stoller said. It doesn't expect to increase the staff significantly.

The idea is to give people of every economic status the information they need during and after cancer.

"Lance had a lot of resources when he was going through his cancer," Stoller said. "We want to be able to provide those same resources to, say, someone in West Virginia."

Exponential growth of any nonprofit group can be hard to handle, said Daniel Borochoff, president of the American Institute of Philanthropy.

It needs strong management, smart planning and wise spending habits. It also needs to protect its image by closely monitoring fund-raisers in its name.

So far, the Lance Armstrong Foundation seems to be handling its success sensibly, Borochoff said. Its administrative costs are low, and it is using its money to invest in programs.

"It sounds like they are positioning themselves well," he said.

Charity Navigator, which evaluates 3,100 nonprofit groups across the country, gives the foundation its highest ranking, four stars.

Garvey gives much of the credit to the foundation's namesake.

"This is a leader who is the real deal," Garvey said.

Armstrong attends fund-raisers and courts major donors, he said. He serves on the President's Cancer Panel and communicates with foundation leaders. He occasionally stops by the foundation office, where he has a mailbox.

Garvey's assessment: "We would not be where we are today if all Lance did was continue to win Tours de France." But a sixth Tour victory on Sunday won't hurt.

"He is doubtless the greatest rider ever in the Tour de France."

TOUR PRESIDENT PATRICE CLERC

LANCE SURPASSED ALL BUT HIS OWN EXPECTATIONS

KIRK BOHLS
American-Statesman Staff

July 25, 2004

PARIS — The morning after his fifth consecutive victory in the Tour de France was assured last July, Lance Armstrong gathered his U.S. Postal team and staff on the train ride to Le Puy de Fou for the start of the triumphant ride toward the fabled Champs-Elysées.

Exhausted but reflective after a grueling race that featured crashes and other brushes with disaster, he wanted no repeat of his narrow, 61-second win over Jan Ullrich.

He delivered a very clear and emotional message.

"I'll come back, better prepared," Armstrong vowed. "It's going to be a lot easier next year."

The 32-year-old Texan proved good on his promise. So good, in fact, that he returned for a record sixth victory, more focused and in better shape and completely dominated the 2004 Tour de France without contradiction from anyone other than a young Italian comer and a strong German understudy to 1997 champion Jan Ullrich.

Six minutes and 19 seconds separated Armstrong and Ullrich's teammate, Andreas Klöden.

Now history separates Lance and anyone else who has ever cycled in the Tour de France. His 'A' game. What began with a telling, second-place time in the prologue in Liege, Belgium, ended with a flurry of four stage wins in five days before Sunday's stirring symbolic ride into the French capital from Montereau where Napoleon won his last battle.

Everyone, it seemed, wanted a memory from the historic conclusion. The Lanterne Rouge, or last-place rider, Jimmy Casper, made a pseudo-attack of the peloton Sunday morning just so he could dig out his digital camera and take a shot of him "leading" Armstrong early in the stage.

Alas, Casper was but a ghost in this race, finishing three hours and 56 minutes in the rear.

At the 13-mile mark — roughly a seventh of the way on this final trip — an upbeat Armstrong was sipping champagne and toasting Postal Director Johan Bruyneel driving the team car alongside.

"Lance brought his 'A' game," said cycling commentator Bob Roll, himself a four-time Tour rider. "He's the strongest guy in the world. The rest of the field turned to ashes and disintegrated."

As the final 147 riders sprinted down the Champs-Elysées for the eight ceremonial laps, public-address announcer Daniel Mangeas, the incessant voice of Paris racing, boomed non-stop for well over an hour.

Armstrong's mother, Linda, wearing a yellow dress, was on hand in the huge grandstand with a yellow canopy shielding the dazzling sunshine. So were his girlfriend Sheryl Crow and cycling buddy Robin Williams.

Even actor Will Smith stopped by amidst the estimated 350,000 of cycling fans who had begun taking their spots four hours earlier.

Scott Coady, a 46-year-old San Franciscan who quit his consultant's job in 2000 to film a documentary of his own month-long Tour adventure in a white rental van,

LANCE ARMSTRONG SHAKES HANDS WITH TEAM CSC'S IVAN BASSO ON THE WINNER'S PODIUM AFTER ARMSTRONG WON HIS SIXTH TOUR DE FRANCE. BASSO IS WEARING A YELLOW BRACELET IN SUPPORT OF THE LANCE ARMSTRONG FOUNDATION FOR CANCER RESEARCH.

was shooting away for another short film to be called *Postcards to Lance*.

Down the road at the Place de la Concorde, hundreds sandwiched around the U.S. Postal bus. Seven-year-old Max Bucksbaum from Chicago and his 4-year-old brother Eli, decked out in full Postal regalia, looked on with their parents.

All just wanted a glimpse of Armstrong, the man who made one of the world's grandest sporting events uniquely American for the past six years.

"He's awesome," said Bill Hancock, who has handled the Final Four for the NCAA for the last 16 years but was moved by the magnitude of Sunday's event. "You can't explain this scene to anyone at home."

The men he passed

It capped a 2,108-mile journey that Armstrong reduced to a three-week parade for the man who sealed his greatness and stamped his name as the only six-time winner in the Tour's illustrious 91-year history.

Armstrong came here in 1999, 21 months removed from testicular, lung and brain cancer, operating out of a revamped mobile home and calling his team the Bad News Bears.

Today with a luxurious, 27-foot-long red, blue and gray bus — complete with a shower and a kitchen — he showed up here a confident, striking figure who has now bettered all the racing titans.

He has topped Eddie "The Cannibal" Merckx, a voracious competitor who won every third race he ever entered with more than 450 career victories and was finally stopped short of six triumphs in 1975 when an enraged spectator lunged at him and kicked him in the liver.

He has eclipsed beloved Frenchman Bernard Hinault, who suffered knee injuries that prevented him from stacking up more than the five titles he claimed over seven years and who has been on hand as a Tour official to shake Lance's hand after each of his career-high five stage wins.

He's one up on Spaniard immortal Miguel Indurain, who lost out to current CSC team director Bjarne Riis in 1996 and saw his final bid for six crowns end at a stage in Indurain's own hometown of Pamplona.

Not even the late Jacques Anquetil could reach six after winning his first at the young age of 22 and four more afterward in the early 1960s.

Armstrong is clearly the greatest cyclist in history

even if he won't afford himself the smugness of admitting he crushed the 2004 field of 187 riders, 40 of whom didn't even reach Paris.

As the French would say, he is Le Meilleur, the King of the Tour.

When asked if he totally dominated the field, Armstrong said, "No. I was remarking to Johan that I hardly, if ever, attacked. But I wouldn't be so bold to call it a domination."

However, there's no other way to describe the way he sucked all the drama out of the race. For the past five years, Armstrong had been the Tour's best climber in the mountain stages and best time trialer, but his all-out charges to the finish line to pass Ivan Basso and Klöden in the Pyrenees and Alps revealed yet another facet to this multiskilled rider.

"For some reason, I'm enjoying the competition more than ever," he said. "To win the sprints is something I've never done before, but I'm having more fun riding a bike than ever."

Ali, Jordan, Lance

The screenplay of his turbulent and triumphant life is in the works with Matt Damon as a likely choice to play the lead. Perhaps it should be titled "Paris in Sprint Time" because Armstrong answered every challenge and appeared as fresh at the end as he did at the start 22 days before.

"He is doubtless the greatest rider ever in the Tour de France," said no less an authority than Tour president Patrice Clerc. "He is proving that."

With his sixth title, Armstrong puts himself on a stage with such international sports legends as heavyweight boxing champion Muhammad Ali and baseball slugger Babe Ruth and soccer icon Pele. All dominated their games and did so with such charisma and swagger that they transcended their sports.

"Eddie Merckx had a higher winning percentage than Lance and won hundreds more races," Roll said. "Wilt Chamberlain scored more points (100) in a game than Michael Jordan ever did, but because of all the championships, Jordan is considered the best of all time."

Jordan, too, dominated and raised the level of his lesser teammates to six NBA titles over a span of eight seasons.

So it was with a similarly strong if less heralded supporting cast that Armstrong has put his name in the

**LANCE ARMSTRONG CYCLES PAST AN AUDIENCE IN
PARIS DURING THE FINAL STAGE OF THE 2004 TOUR.**

**THE PRESS SURROUNDS LANCE ARMSTRONG
AS THE U.S. POSTAL SERVICE TEAM MAKES A CIRCLE
AROUND THE CHAMPS-ELYSÉES ON JULY 25, 2004.**

DEBORAH CANNON/AUSTIN AMERICAN-STATESMAN

"Nobody showed up."

BILL STAPLETON, ARMSTRONG'S AGENT

history books.

Both sought out motivation in the least of insults and unkind words, whether real or perceived. Armstrong, too, had his doubters before this event began and detractors during, like three-time champion Greg LeMond, during because Lance alternately seemed so vulnerable in 2003 or too powerful in 2004.

However, he crushed his competitors in a February time trial in Portugal, then swept through the Tour of Georgia in April as a warmup for his ultimate triumph.

Nobody showed up

This, after all, is the most driven of cyclists, a man still reaching his peak, a man who is so meticulous in his training that he rides on Christmas Day and religiously weighs himself months before the Tour to ensure he's not so much as a single nacho over his desired weight.

Such was his preparation for this race that he showed up in Belgium on July 3 as fit as he has ever been and at peace after his divorce from wife Kristin and with his budding romance with a rock star.

All he wanted to do was have some fun, and he certainly did that.

"He had this race won since it finished last year," said CSC's Bobby Julich, a former Armstrong teammate. "He committed himself to winning this race the day after he won his fifth. I've always said Lance is going to win seven, and that was three years ago. I still think he'll put the record so far out of reach, no one will come close. He's well on his way."

Once the race began, Armstrong served notice immediately that this year's Tour would offer no repeat of last July. He whittled off all but 22 seconds of a nine-minute deficit in two Pyrenees stages, then put on the yellow jersey at Villard de Lans and never took it off for the final six days.

"Nobody showed up," shrugged Bill Stapleton, Armstrong's agent and chief executive of Tailwind Sports, which owns Armstrong's team.

It was no contest from emphatic start to glorious finish before millions along country roads and up steep mountain climbs.

He came on a mission, he toyed with the contenders, outclassed a surging German and an aspiring Italian, and in the end emerged as the campionissimo, the champion of champions.

ARMSTRONG MAKES HISTORY WITH SIXTH TOUR VICTORY

Lance savors Sunday's final stage with glass of champagne in the saddle

SUZANNE HALLIBURTON
American-Statesman Staff

July 25, 2004

PARIS, France — The smooth cobblestones of the Champs-Elysées have been the scene for all 91 finish lines of the Tour de France. As soon as the peloton passes through the blue arrival arch, an ornate podium is quickly wheeled midway between the Place de la Concorde and the Arc d'Triomphe on this famous boulevard. Hundreds of thousands of fans applaud as the champion of the world's grandest bike race is crowned, and the other coveted jerseys are awarded.

Yet Sunday's uniquely French celebration against sun-splashed skies was more special than any Tour closing soiree in history.

After all, in a century of racing, no rider besides Austin's Lance Armstrong had ever won six Tour titles, much less claimed them all in a row.

Armstrong wore a broad smile as he acknowledged the roars of the crowd, many of whom waved Texas flags. He then accepted the trophies and kisses from the traditional Tour sponsors.

"I think the biggest memory I'll take away from this Tour is taking the final step to the podium," the 32-year-old Armstrong said beforehand. He made no public comments after the race.

Bernard Hinault, one of four men to win the Tour five times, zipped up Armstrong's yellow jersey for a final time, and the mayor of Paris presented him with another stuffed lion from Credit Lyonnais, the Tour's most prominent sponsor.

Hinault, known as "The Badger" during his five victories, had predicted before the Tour started that Armstrong would claim six, breaking the record owned by five riders. However, many others believed Germany's

Jan Ullrich would finally beat his archrival after the two ended up only 61 seconds a part a year ago.

"No worries," Hinault told reporters. "Lance is by far the biggest perfectionist and the best rider of the Tour today."

That showed, especially in Armstrong's head-to-head battle with Ullrich, who couldn't keep up in the early mountain stages and finished fourth overall, 8 minutes, 50 seconds out of first place. It was the first time Ullrich, the 1997 champion, did not finish on the podium with the top three riders. Instead, Ullrich's teammate Andreas Klöden finished second to Armstrong, 6:19 out of first place.

"I don't think this has really sunk in yet," said Chris Carmichael, Armstrong's longtime private coach. "Lance is about the here and now. He sucks the marrow out of the day. He's about living like there's no tomorrow. That's a great way to live life."

Carmichael said Armstrong had two major wakeup calls in his career. One was his cancer diagnosis in 1996. The other was last year's narrow win over Ullrich, the sixth tightest in Tour history. It inspired him to start working on this year's Tour 12 months ago.

In picking up his sixth championship, Armstrong was the most dominant of his career, almost as overwhelming as Eddy Merckx, the Belgian who won five Tours and is widely thought to be the best rider in history.

"I think Lance impressed everyone — the riders, the journalists and of course, the fans," said Denis Descamps, a spokesman for ASO, the company that operates the Tour.

"He spoke French, and we really appreciated that. It's

ROBBIE MCEWAN (LEFT) WEARING THE SPRINTER'S JERSEY, LANCE
ARMSTRONG, RICHARD VIRENQUE (SECOND FROM RIGHT), WEARING
THE MOUNTAIN JERSEY AND VLADIMIR KARPETS (RIGHT), WEARING THE
BEST YOUNG RIDER JERSEY, CELEBRATE AFTER THE 2004 RACE.

"He worked this race like crazy."

ARMSTRONG'S GIRLFRIEND SHERYL CROW

**SHERYL CROW WAS ON HAND TO SUPPORT
LANCE ARMSTRONG THROUGHOUT THE 2004 TOUR.**

"This year Lance has been straightforward and so has his team. They haven't made one mistake all Tour."

AUSTRALIAN RIDER ROBBIE McEWAN

the first time we've seen a rider so strong. He was best in the time trials, best in the mountains, best in the flat stages. He controlled everything. He was like Eddy Merckx."

Armstrong won six stages — five individual and one in the team time trial to go along with runner-up finishes in the opening prologue and first mountain stage in the Pyrenees. It was widely known then that Armstrong allowed Basso, his good friend, to ease ahead on the ascent to La Mongie to take victory to help the young Italian deal with the terminal illness of his mother.

Conversely, Merckx, in winning his first Tour back in 1968, won seven stages, six of them individual. "It's incredible that he's won six times," said Australian rider Robbie McEwen, who won the Tour's green sprinting jersey for the second straight year. "He's been the best prepared and the strongest rider. I can't see any reason he can't come back and win seven in a row.

"This year, Lance has been straightforward and so has his team. They haven't made one mistake all Tour. For them, it all went like clockwork."

The U.S. Postal team had an intimate dinner at the Chateau De Germigney on Saturday night to celebrate their accompishments. The team finished second overall to T-Mobile in the team classification, with Jose Azevedo, the team's newest member, finishing fifth overall. Armstrong said at the midway point of the Tour that historians would document that Postal had the strongest team effort in the race's history.

Sunday morning, all the teams took a high-speed train from Besancon to Montereau, a village southeast of Paris, to start Stage 20.

As per tradition, Armstrong was allowed to ride first out of the village as Tour Director Jean Marie Leblanc waved the red flag to start the stage. For the first few miles, the riders joked around, with some even taking out portable cameras to take photos of themselves to commemorate the occasion.

Then they arrived in Paris, shortly after 4 p.m. local time, to ride the eight laps of the Champs-Elysées. Teams with riders in contention for the green jersey awarded to the top sprinter tried to set them up for a stage victory.

Belgium's Tom Boonen crossed first. The stage is largely ceremonial, but for the sprinters, it's a victory that will be one of their greatest memories.

Then, Hollywood took over the French party for Armstrong's best day of his career.

Actor Will Smith, who was in town to promote his movie *I Robot*, made an appearance on the podium, as Armstrong's entourage, including rock-star girlfriend Sheryl Crow and good friend Robin Williams, the actor and comedian, applauded from the yellow-covered grandstand.

"He worked this race like crazy," Crow said.

Her first big hit, "All I Want to do is Have Some Fun," serenaded the teams as they took a final stroll along the Champs-Elysées.

Linda Armstrong, Lance's mother, was in attendance. But his three children stayed back in Austin.

Armstrong will stay one more week in Europe, riding criteriums in the Netherlands, Germany and the Czech Republic. He'll be back in Austin in early August to see son Luke and twin daughters Isabelle and Grace for the first time in three months.

He'll start working on next year's cycling season starting in November, deciding in December which races will be on his itinerary. It's likely he'll come back to France next July, and it's likely he'll continue to suck the life out of every day.

127

Special thanks to the staff of the
Austin American-Statesman *for*
their tireless coverage of Lance Armstrong
and his six Tour de France victories.